No Time To Wander

The financial compass for young Americans

Paul Nourigat

FarBeyond Publishing

Credits

Illustrator - James Beihl
A multi-talented sequential artist based in New York.

Research - Nick Nourigat
Market research, compilation and documentation.
A great sense for what matters.

Book Layout - Irene Sprang
Outstanding graphical, visual and collaborative skills.

Technical Charts - Crandall, Pierce & Company
This Chicago area firm develops charts for the financial industry, creating powerful visuals which highlight trends and the causes-and-effects of various market events and personal actions, from a large number of data points. They were kind enough to customize charts to help me communicate a series of key messages regarding the effects of education on employment and compensation (Chapter 4) and the performance history of various investment portfolio configurations against the effects of inflation (Chapter 9).

Executive Editor - Lisa Nourigat
Candid perspectives and thoughtful opinions.

Text and Illustrations Copyright © 2013 FarBeyond Publishing LLC
Manufactured in USA

FarBeyond Publishing LLC
No Time To Wander: the financial compass for young Americans
978-1-936872-08-4

Library of Congress Control Number: 2013941066

Reproduction or distribution of this book, its content or images in any format is expressly forbidden without prior written consent of author. Please support author rights and report any violations of copyright law.

Contents

Foreword By John Mitchell, Economist i

Introduction 1

1   You, Inc. . . . . taking control 3

2   Reality . . . . evolution of work 15

3   Renewal . . . . opportunities on the horizon. . . 27

4   Finding A Job. . . . . winning strategies and tactics. . 41

5   Protecting A Job. . . . . counter-intuitive measures 67

6   Winning The Race?. . . . . expense strategies. 87

7   Choose Any Door . . . . good, bad and ugly debt. 103

8   Tradeoffs . . . . the impact of savings. 119

9   The Investment Carnival . . wealth magnification 131

10   It's Complicated . . . . relationships and money 149

11   Beyond You . . . . practical compassion 163

12   Jeopardy . . . . life's traps 171

13   The Power of Struggle. . . . . success factors. 199

Bibliography 209

Resources Guide 215

Index 223

Foreword
John Mitchell, Economist

A primer for one's economic life is perhaps the best way to describe Paul Nourigat's No Time to Wander. We usually enter the world of work, go through school, and make decisions that have long term implications with little guidance. I was fortunate to grow up in a household where views were shaped by the Great Depression of the 1930's. At 16 one was expected to work summers and on college vacations. My first career was in fast food at minimum wage where I learned to show up, work hard, get along with teammates, while putting out great ice cream treats. Jobs as a lifeguard, an assistant athletic trainer, a policeman, an economics professor and a bank economist followed. The world was different in the last century when many decisions were made for you in regard to things like retirement and medical insurance; risks posed by the eternal life of e-mails and Facebook postings did not exist. It would have been nice to have a guide like No Time To Wander to encourage more careful deliberations.

In 2013, nearly five years after "The Great Recession" ended, employment has yet to reach its prerecession peak, the average duration of unemployment is nearly 10 months, and teenage unemployment is in double digits. The optimism about the future has been dimmed. Young people are entering a world of work that is competitive, and this book offers tips and guides about interviews and the search for employment that may not be obvious to many people. The author points out that "every job offers an opportunity to learn something new about a company, an industry, other people, new tasks and most importantly yourself." The style of the book is engaging and gets people to think in terms of their brand and its attributes, creation and presentation.

One's fortunes can depend on skills and experience acquired from decisions made in one's 20's and 30's, impacting retirement options decades in the future. No Time to Wander provides insights into sources of information for some of those decisions and contains illustrations of the implications of things like getting an early start on savings for retirement. As we go through life we are confronted with new decisions about spending, saving, investing, borrowing, renting versus buying, and acquiring insurance. The book contains non-technical definitions and examples to assist readers, presented by someone not trying to sell you anything. For many, I suspect this material was not covered at home or in courses outside of business programs. Although I remember having to fill out a 1040 Tax Return in 8th Grade, I do not think my daughters ever had to do that in their educational paths through college.

The book is a guide written by someone with extensive experience in observing people's behavior. Things that come with age such as the importance of a support network from the Doctor to the Insurance Agent and a Financial Planner are discussed, as are risks in terms of Tax, Health and Behavioral Jeopardy. The narrative elaborates on those mistakes and misfortunes that can disrupt our lives, but reminds us of the things that we can control and our resilience. We learn by doing with both successes and failures; No Time To Wander: the financial compass for young Americans provides insights and information in an entertaining way that can help increase the reader's successes.

John W. Mitchell

John Mitchell received his B.A. degree from Williams College and his M.S. and Ph.D. degrees from the University of Oregon. He was a professor of economics at Boise State University for 13 years prior to becoming Chief Economist of U.S. Bancorp from July of 1983-1998 and throughout the west from 1998 until 2007. Today, John speaks to large groups around the country, continuing to offer economic updates and perspectives in a style which many can embrace.

Introduction

Reflect back on your graduation from school. You were relieved to be finished and proud of yourself ... and then you had to move on. The world only celebrates success for a very short time, right?

Reality hits fast. When moving from student/absorb mode to adult/produce mode, new dimensions of life present unexpected challenges. This phase has always been challenging, yet with increased global competition, automation, and the recession's effect on jobs and real wages, young Americans today are facing a very difficult economic environment. Many feel a sense of despair. However, there's truly a rainbow ahead, if you know where to look.

I respect the uniqueness of people, yet also recognize what we have in common. Regardless of heritage, race, political party, relationship status, gender, religious beliefs, or educational level, the essentials in this book apply to all Americans. I won't tell you how to live your life, but will explain in clear terms how you can significantly improve your financial posture in any environment, in order to pursue the life you want.

Many millions of people will wander and struggle in the years ahead, while others will taste early success only to have it pulled away through their errors or misfortunes. Things can be better for you. There will be incredible opportunities if you position yourself for success. Over the next ten years, planning and effectively navigating your financial journey will make the difference between surviving and thriving.

What's a "Young American"?

Ok, let's get something out of the way.
I'd be starting off poorly if I characterized you as a "Millennial",
"twenty something", "GenX", or "GenY". So I won't.

Marketing types seem fixated on classifying you
and characterizing your behaviors, attitudes and tendencies
in some broad common form. I know that's bunk.

Truth is, I fumbled with how to be true to my readers
and yet still make it clear "who" I am writing for. I use the term
"Young Americans" to refer to adults who have
moved beyond school - at any level - and are seeking long term
independence and financial freedom over the next decade.

My messaging throughout the book is free of politics,
corporate interests and value statements. You'll have come
from a very different place than the reader somewhere else,
who is also reading this paragraph right now.
Your desire to build a secure and comfortable future
is our common ground.

"You, Incorporated"

Can you imagine owning a company in your name? We'll call it "You, Inc." and people will pay you just to be you. What if you were paid more money if people liked your look, and received bonus compensation if you chose to work smarter and harder than others?

That company exists right now. "You, Inc" is your brand which speaks to every person you meet. It is sized up within seconds of every greeting, from a distance at a social event, or when walking by in the mall. It certainly exists where you're working, or in the interview while seeking your next job. Your brand image commands attention (good and bad) and garners varying levels of respect and compensation. Do you care enough about your financial success to modify your brand image?

A very cool thing about America's economy is that its "free market" design moves money to the places which people value the most. Neither the President, the Governor, nor your family members can dictate the price that you will command in the marketplace. Essentially, if you have a product, *"You, Inc."*, which someone values, they'll pay a higher rate than a lesser product, "Them, Inc.".

If *You, Inc.* wants to prosper financially, it must identify and align with the products, services and styles which people and companies value. Whether you're an engineer, a retail worker, a doctor, or an entertainer, you have the opportunity to maneuver *You, Inc.* into position to command top dollar and job security within the industry and job you've chosen. You're more in control than you think.

Before we get into essential financial topics, let's jump into personal branding. This chapter will show you how to establish and enhance your personal brand to position *You, Inc.* for as big of a success as you choose to define.

SO, WHO DO YOU WANT TO BE?

This book isn't about "wealth creation" or my vision for your life. Instead, it focuses on your vision and the financial requirements to achieve your vision. If you're thinking "I have no clue where I'll be, who I'll be with, and what my financial position will be in the future", relax. You're in good company. For most of us, day-to-day life is a dust storm of activities and unknowns, making it difficult to step back to reflect and imagine. The beauty is that your "vision" for yourself can be whatever you choose, over any timeframe, as long as the vision is of great interest to you, somewhat relevant to others, and achievable. Then your activities and financial plan to support that vision can be constructed.

Truth is, in my youth I was not a great planner. I showed up to most things, literally falling into good and bad situations. Through some luck and many nice people along the way, I had chances to redeem myself in order to experience enough success to finally recognize the positive cause-and-effect of my actions, including the benefits of planning. Here is a snapshot of how my vision evolved during my early adult life:

- At 23, upon graduation ... "Earn $25,000 and have some fun"
- At 25, ... "Get married, retire by 40, build wealth for security, then focus on other things."
- At 44 ... "Positively impact my community and society while protecting my family's finances.

I was clearly driven by financial independence. My parents were good people who worked hard but struggled with financial concepts and disciplines, ultimately leading to an implosion of their finances and marriage. That was a yard sale I did not enjoy watching, motivating me to reach a better zone early in life. This is not the approach I'm recommending to you, but an example of what's possible. I'm 54 now, and I work for fun.

Life isn't about finding yourself.
Life is about creating yourself.

... George Bernard Shaw

BUILDING YOUR VISION

There are certain aspects of life I couldn't imagine in my early adult years. Most things were brand new to me upon graduation and my eyes were wide open to the new world I was experiencing. I'm glad I did not try to craft my entire life plan early on, as the world around me changed and many new experiences altered my perspectives.

Allow yourself the comfort of knowing you can reset your vision multiple times in life. With those periodic resets, you can revise the required plan to confidently achieve your vision, rather than hard-coding your destiny. You simply do not know enough about yourself or the world around you in your early adult years, but opportunities will multiply if you keep the door open.

Sometimes we feel pressured to complete our vision because others pronounce their grand plans and accomplishments. Whatever. Trust me, there is a nice middle ground to planning and it resides comfortably between too little (fail) and too much (fail). A helpful planning approach in your early years is KISS (Keep It Simple Silly), but do it.

Before we begin building the *You, Inc.* brand, let's begin creating your vision, by establishing your hopes and dreams that form your vision and guide your supporting financial goals. Following is an approach I encourage you to take right now, knowing that you can refine it later. This will not hurt. Get a sheet of paper and a pencil and spend 5 minutes on this small, but important, step. Flip this page over and let's get to it.

BUILDING YOUR VISION

HOPES AND DREAMS

One year vision (what do I most want to accomplish?)

1)

2)

3)

Five year vision (same drill, farther out on the horizon)

1)

2)

3)

4)

Twenty year vision (same drill, much farther out)

1)

2)

3)

4)

5)

<u>Themes To Consider</u>
Family, Health, Financial, Career,
Community, Spiritual, Academic, Athletic, Creative
(Printable version at www.MarvelsOfMoney.org/adults)

LIFE VISION EXERCISE

For this exercise, create a worksheet for yourself on a blank piece of paper, or use the print-ready version (link at base of last page). Write down the headings and numbering as shown on the example on the left. Then, consider the many dimensions of life, including family, health, financial, career, community, spiritual, academic, athletic, artistic, etc.

- One year from now - What accomplishments would you like to reflect back upon?
- Five years out - Same thing, imagine looking back in five years. Note your top three or four desired accomplishments within that time frame, building upon your one year plan with additional items.
- Twenty years out on the horizon - Bottom 1/3 of the page. What are four or five additional life accomplishments over the next twenty years you would like to look back on someday? If you struggle on this, you're not alone. The farther out, the more obscure things become.

Ok, now as you scan that list, can you see what is most important to you? Place a checkmark next to every item needing financial strength. For most of us, financial strength is the foundation to achieving life goals; although not the end-game, it is usually the means to an end. Given that importance, let's get real about how to build your brand so it balances your unique interests and preferences with the behaviors and choices that facilitate financial success.

With this approach, your efforts around financial essentials are well directed and your motivations become self-fulfilling. This is you telling *You, Inc.* what is most important. From this point forward, we will reflect on your vision over and over as it will guide many of the strategies I'll recommend.

YOUR BRAND CHECKLIST

Refining the following items will enhance your pay scale and job security, improving your financial capacity.

Integrity - Honorable virtues, such as truthfulness and empathy are more important to employers than your skills or educational level. Sure, there are some jobs which don't let you in the door without certain credentials, yet because employers have plenty of resumes with comparable skills and education, they're focusing on the character of the person. That's the difference they find between great long-term employees and those who do not last. Employees who do not last present risks and expenses to the employer which are bad for business.

Your look - Does your image attract, or scare off the people you want to associate with? That means clothing, hair, makeup, jewelry, etc. No, we're not talking cloning the perfect employee, but consider the importance of compatibility for each unique environment. Your look is something you can tweak on demand to improve your fit within an environment. If you want to broaden your job options to enhance your financial posture, to achieve your life mission, a tattoo of some ancient cult symbol on your forehead is probably not a good idea. Image matters, and although what you feel is important, so is what others feel about you.

Your archive - You know that web page that has the funny picture of you doing something dumb that one night? And what about your blog where you posted a rant when you were really ticked off about something? Most of us have been there, doing something or saying something which was really funny or seemingly important at the time, but now looks stupid. The difference in this decade is that many young Americans have developed web personas - often unknowingly - offering windows into indiscretions which in decades past would have been buried for good. People forgive and forget, but the web doesn't, which can be catastrophic to moving on to your next life chapter.

Employers and clients use online resources to assess the character of people they choose to do business with. Whether you like it or not, cleaning up your market-facing image goes beyond today's outfit selection. If your online stuff does not support your future vision, clean it up and assure that your new stuff becomes all they see.

Your Associations - Our associations with people, places and activities define us. Scan your vision document again, then consider what you've been doing and who you've been hanging out with. How well does it align with your hopes and dreams? Ultimately, your priorities may have you pushing *You, Inc.* through relationship and situational changes.

Your Balance - It's cool to be driven to excellence, but not at the expense of the world around you or your own long-term health. As you review your various hopes and dreams, does your list feel balanced? People with a range of experiences and who are interested in more than one thing are both fascinating and effective. Their life balance gives them critical intellectual cross-pollination, puts them more at peace with themselves and offers important coping mechanisms (think fallback plan when something breaks down).

Things break down at some point for even those single minded, ultra-successful people. When the world around them changes, they're devastated because of their singular focus and dependency on one thing. This book was written for the other 99.9% of Americans who want a well balanced life while they're achieving financial success. Conversely, the more common reason for imbalance is dilution. Many smart and "normal" people fall down on their personal brand unintentionally, having loaded up so many things, duties and relationships that they become overwhelmed and do nothing well. Just as balance disallows the unhealthy singular focus, it provides a guide to avoid over-committing.

Walking the Talk - Great personal branding is not about creating a facade, but defining who you want to be, developing in a purposeful direction and projecting it most effectively. The world's full of people talking big and not delivering. You will rise above the vast majority simply through discipline and delivering on the promise of your brand, whatever that might be.

Brand Alignment - When working with employers, coworkers and customers, everyone is constantly sized up for compatibility. Most people in our country have broadened their view of compatibility as our society has matured; the free flow of information and mobility of people have broken down many stereotypes. Still, even the most liberal thinker out there will size you up and "choose you" given their confidence that you will fit into their environment and help them accomplish something, producing more benefits than risk. Are you likely to deliver results worth the price of the things they do not like about you or are uncomfortable with?

I'm not sure if it is "fair", but it's how nature has wired us. The old saying "birds of a feather flock together" is a natural phenomenon which humans are constantly refining.

The Bottom Line - With all the bad news in the world and with our economy struggling, will personal brand development matter? Well, there are tons of things outside of our control which can hurt us, so we'd better control the things we can. You can significantly impact your financial success by developing and projecting character and technical strengths, while maintaining awareness of your outward "packaging".

By knowing what's going on, and where we're headed, you'll be better positioned for greater options than the people who wait to be told what to do or "hope" for things to get better. Now that you've considered your vision, along with how your personal brand can affect it, let's peer into the most relevant workplace trends which will affect us over the next ten years.

> PERSPECTIVE: LABOR TRANSITION
>
> Forbes' Magazine's John Bruner reported that manufacturing jobs have fallen from 32% of American workers in 1953 to 9% in 2011.

Reality

When you're experiencing your first negative economic period, it feels like the sky is falling as bad news abounds. The economic problems of the day are compounded by negative headlines, with complainers complaining about the things that their neighbors and coworkers are complaining about. It becomes a self-perpetuating trap which limits many people's hopes and ambitions.

In fact, economic contractions occur are every 10-20 years, in an almost natural cycle. Parts of the economy, such as home prices, go up too far and then swing downward when people are unable or unwilling to pay the higher prices. Some people win, some people lose, and then the cycle begins anew. I'm oversimplifying, but that is the essence of economic and market cycles.

Twenty-somethings lived through the double-blow of the Internet bubble bursting in 2001 and the great recession of 2008/2009. Americans had spent beyond their means, borrowed as if they would always have a job and assumed home prices would always rise. The financial collapses affected the psyche of American families and eroded millions of young Americans' confidence. Entering an economic contraction from a position of strength is the key to surviving what will otherwise be a long and hard struggle for financial security. Those are big words for people just trying to buy a meal or find a job. I can't change the facts of life, but a good understanding of where we're at and where we're going will help you to capitalize on the good times ahead.

Dealing with reality straight-on is the key to survival and long-term success. As you'll see, there are both challenges and opportunities on the horizon. This chapter provides a chronology of the changes which have affected the evolution of our job market. From there, we'll move into the significant economic renewal on the horizon and the tactics you can implement to succeed in this new job market.

WHAT HAPPENED TO WORK?

Let's consider how work has evolved to its present state, so you're prepared for the curious dynamics of the modern workforce.

Automation - Computerization of administrative and repetitive tasks, coupled with robotics and automated manufacturing systems, have reduced, or in some cases, eliminated the demand for many classifications of workers. This is why many corporations report significant profit improvements following difficult economic periods. As employees are laid off due to lack of demand for a company's products or services, a leaner staff stays on to keep the ship afloat. During that time, as the economy improves, the fewer employees "find a way" to get the jobs done using new systems and process improvements.

The resulting efficiencies present the greatest risk to employees whose jobs are highly redundant, or where the process is fairly static. At-risk positions will increase in the years ahead, as certain professional jobs will be displaced with artificial intelligence systems. While improved corporate productivity is crucial to the viability of most U.S. companies, it comes at the expense of millions of American workers. Before you totally freak out, stick with me and understand the balance of what we're dealing with.

Power Shift - In decades past, America's economic dominance was fed by ambition, ample labor and natural resources, backed by one of the most advanced economies in the world. Imperfect, sure, yet far above most other countries.

As other countries' sophistication and economic power increased, America's power base was diluted. Industries which provided solid jobs to many Americans were lost to foreign competition willing to do the same job for 10% of the cost of American wages and benefits.

Ask yourself: If you owned an American company struggling to compete and survive, would you take advantage of significantly lower production costs in order to stay in business? Put another way, if you had to give away some jobs to foreign workers, in order to save jobs for your other American workers, would you? That's a dilemma most American leaders have dealt with for years.

Shipping out your job - Interestingly, "outsourcing" jobs did not start with foreign labor competition, as many assume. The concept is rooted right here in the good ol' USA. At one time, companies did just about everything themselves, hiring workers to accomplish every needed task to run the company. Then, the concept of specialization evolved and companies emerged to do "one thing" really well. These specialist companies offered enhanced quality and efficiency (cost reduction) to companies who weren't great at those unique tasks. From this phenomenon, outsourcing was born and became a standard tactic required for most American leaders to keep their jobs.

Consider computer software. Just twenty years ago, large companies had droves of programmers banging away at keyboards and creating custom computer code to help run their operations. Then, as the speed of technological improvement hastened, their programs had to be frequently recoded to run on the new technologies being introduced. Because they were only doing this for their own company, programming each new program just one-time, it was very hard for programmers to deliver something of high quality in a timely and efficient way. As a result, companies were falling behind in their ability to deliver good products to their clients as their business had become increasingly dependent upon those computer programs. Recognizing this, specialized companies emerged to develop single software programs which could be used by many companies, offering a lower cost and proven performance, thus improving quality and speed to market.

Outsourcing is now a standard staffing strategy. Before you get all persnickety about the concept of outsourcing, consider the food cart where you might buy lunch. Do you think that young food cart operator grew the vegetables used in the stir-fry, or fed the animal which produced the meat for the sandwich? Rarely. They're scrambling every morning to buy their ingredients from specialists, update their signage, prepare their meals and greet their customers.

Even consumers tap outsourcing when they decide whether to change the oil in their car, or drive it into the bay of a oil-change specialist and get it done in 30 minutes. Now, great organizations challenge themselves by asking the question "What makes sense to do in-house, and what makes sense to be done by a third party specialist?" So outsourcing is a good thing, right? Well, yes it is, although it is not cool for employees competing with specialists for their job. Nor is it comfortable for our country, as we have good people on the sidelines out of work, collecting unemployment benefits as we ship their jobs overseas. We must learn to adapt, for beyond the fundamental good reasoning for local outsourcing, competitive foreign labor sources continue to emerge and displace certain jobs. That pattern can reverse directions, given changes in labor costs, energy costs, or politics.

At one time, most companies would not dream of moving a job overseas, due to "Made in the USA" loyalty, quality control concerns, and speed to market. It was overly difficult to ship a task or role overseas, and remain in concert with the balance of the company's "onshore" tasks. What happened and why will this labor outsourcing trend continue?

Global Politics - Political leaders eliminated many trade barriers, as they believed a more open global economy, and the resulting international commerce would be beneficial to all. Thus a foreign company, shipping a product into the USA, would no longer need to pay an expensive "tariff" (trade barrier) on their products, which had rendered them uncompetitive in years past. This is but one example of a systemic change which opened up global competition, which in turn put pressure on American companies to produce products and services that were as good and/or priced better than the new competition.

In some cases, this environment improved American companies' ability to ship products overseas as foreign markets opened up, which was clearly the objective of the politicians driving for an global open market. Yet, inequities exist, as countries do not always play nice with their interpretation of free trade.

Education - America began training the world, and sharing our intellectual capital with peoples of all countries. This was driven by the compassion to help others, and the tuition premiums paid to schools by out-of-state/international students. Regardless of how you might feel about this, we have trained the people who will train the other people who will create competitive processes and production practices which will take jobs from Americans.

Education also comes in the form of training others how to use the technologies developed in the U.S. and foreign markets. So American companies profit from selling a product to another country, training them on using the product, which is then used to create products which ultimately compete with the country who sold the stuff to them. The automation and sophistication of many foreign workforces can be traced to American education and training programs.

Mobility - Improved inter-continental transportation allows for rapid and safe passage to and from America. We've benefited from the technical talent, cost/benefit, and work ethic of many foreign workers throughout our history. Beyond undocumented laborers, foreign labor is controlled through work visa programs which should throttle the flow of temporary labor up and down based upon the staffing needs of corporate America.

Add our immigration process to this mobility discussion, as the U.S. attempts to regulate the inflow of new citizens who desperately want to leave their country for the land of promise. Yeah, as bad as we think things are, we don't have lines of people waiting to leave our country, but rather the opposite. We'll learn later why that is such a good thing.

Communications - The greatest change to spur global competition was the speed of computing and communicating, magnified through the Internet. The barriers to offshore labor dropped significantly when a person in one country could receive a set of instructions electronically from a supervisor in another country, work on the project and deliver back the results without a personal conversation. As sterile as that seems, work might be done overnight thanks to time zone differences, while we're still sleeping, at 20% of the cost of the on-shore labor. Ouch.

It's tough to compete with that, yet major transformations like this have occurred throughout history. At the turn of the last century, what do you think the drivers of horse carriages had to say about Henry Ford's vision for families having cars? Just 30 years ago, how do you think accountants felt when they learned that 60% of accounting would be automated by computerization within 10 years? There is always a way to capitalize on change, rather than hide from it or fight it. We'll get there in the coming chapters.

The Hangover - As labor has been radically transformed, employment woes for young Americans are compounded by economic declines, as youth compete for jobs in a market crowded with proven veterans. As you turn the page, let's look at how unemployment and compensation are affected by educational levels and economic cycles.

When one door closes, another opens;
but we often look so long and regretfully upon the closed door
that we do not see the one that has opened for us.

... Alexander Graham Bell

Education and Employment
Civilian Labor Force 25 Years and Older

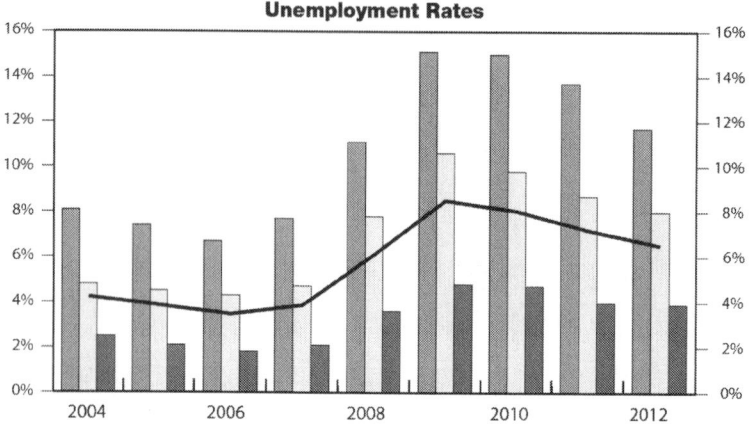

No High School Diploma
High School Graduates, No College

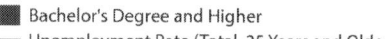
Bachelor's Degree and Higher
— Unemployment Rate (Total, 25 Years and Older)

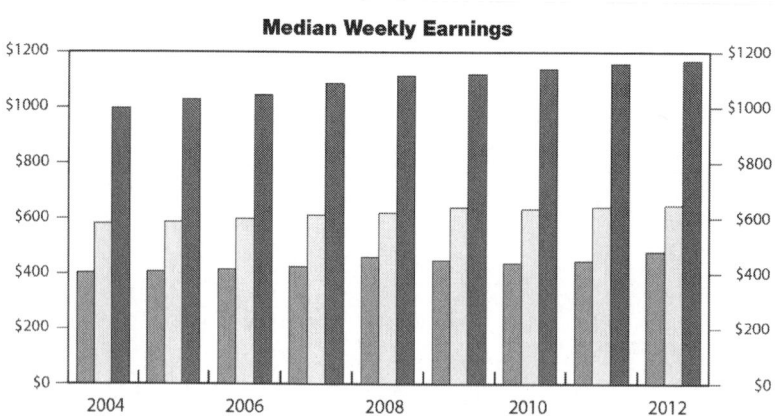

All data is year end.
Sources: Bureau of Labor Statistics • Copyright 2013 Crandall, Pierce & Company • All rights reserved.

The information presented herein was compiled from sources believed to be reliable. It is intended for illustrative purposes only, and is furnished without responsibility for completeness or accuracy. Past performance does not guarantee future results.

As you scan the charts on the preceding page, you see the effect of education on unemployment (upper chart) and compensation level (lower chart). Anyone wondering whether they should finish or invest in their education can be quickly motivated by each of the two charts.

What you also see is the natural cycle of unemployment and its correlation with our economy: as our economy was flying high in 2006, employers could not fill their vacant jobs fast enough, thus the lowered unemployment rate, (line in upper chart) compared with 2009's screeching halt to hiring as the economy tanked and employers pulled back based upon lower projected sales.

The advertised unemployment numbers are understated, they exclude many capable working age citizens who had given up looking for work, or those whose unemployment benefits had run out. This is called "shadow unemployment".

Although the 2008/2009 great recession, and the years following it have been very difficult, 1982 was like this, with unemployment rates exceeding the recent unemployment peaks. How have young Americans broken through difficult periods like this before? The same way people will this cycle and the next, and the next. They'll dig in, be resourceful, humble themselves to reality, while preparing for the upswing. For some, that means going back to school to attain their abandoned degree while things are slow. For those with their desired educational level, it may mean accepting a job which is less than optimal, to "get by" for now. For everyone, it means being really smart about personal finances as I'll outline throughout the balance of this book.

Let's shift gears now, moving from these transformational challenges into the next chapter where we'll focus on significant positive developments on the horizon and how you can capitalize on the renewal that lies ahead.

CHAPTER 3
Renewal

Renewal

Beyond the doom and gloom during the low points of each economic cycle, there is always the promise of tomorrow, given the history of our economy. Let's consider the forces which will fuel this decade's economic renewal. Understanding this can motivate us during the tough times, while offering a preparatory window into the future.

Demographics - Interestingly, the productivity improvements and labor outsourcing referenced in the last chapter arrived a tad early, as our economy entered a mild recession in 2001 and nasty recession in 2008, and well before the anticipated effects of baby boomers aging out of the workforce. Elders' deferred their retirements given their financial struggles or desire to stay engaged. Ultimately, as the infamous baby boom hits its stride, death, incapacity and voluntary retirement will suck life out of the American workforce and replenishment will be required. Georgetown University's 2013 study, "Recovery: job growth and education requirements through 2020", projects 55 million job vacancies, of which 31 million will come from boomer retirements.

The opportunity? Our aging workforce will naturally make room for younger employees, as immigration, efficiencies and sourcing strategies will only partially fill the gap. We'll need young and middle aged people to step into action. As you consider the unemployment and compensation charts at the end of Chapter 2, you'll recall the profound impact of education; many of the jobs you will learn about in the coming chapters require an educated workforce. If you're educated, you're in good shape and if not, you'll probably want to be.

Immigration - It's naturally disconcerting when you're looking for a job and there is talk about immigration. Consider that immigration is not simply about the compassionate accommodation of foreigners.

Throughout America's history, immigrants have accepted the most difficult jobs, bringing a level of industriousness not found with Americans who are so comfortable with life that they're disinterested in "lesser jobs". Immigrants also bring insights from throughout the world to broaden our views and our intellect.

We will prosper from new ideas, new companies, an industrious workforce, and a diverse society which is reasonably regulated. If I'm an economic chef, these are the ingredients for the recipe to create a boom for our society for the next 100 years. But only if it can be managed properly. We should all applaud a well designed and tightly administered immigration process, which welcomes and integrates an appropriate number of newcomers to our communities to enhance the vibrancy and vitality of our country. Without immigration to America, where would we be now?

> PERSPECTIVE: BEYOND CHEAP LABOR
>
> A fascinating study was conducted by researchers at Harvard Medical School, identifying the positive financial impact of immigrants. They noted the average age for Hispanic immigrants (the largest immigrant group) is 27, compared with non-Hispanic white US citizen's age of 47. Thanks to their tax dollars, such youthful immigration resulted in a $115 billion Medicare surplus, compared to a $28 billion deficit for the American-born population. This surplus comes at a time of great concern over the solvency of Medicare, the healthcare security blanket for most aging Americans. The study concludes " Encouraging a steady flow of young immigrants would help offset the aging of the US population and the health care financing challenge that it presents."

Consider the opportunities which will arise from the challenges of blending people with such different cultures, languages and resources, into a concerted team environment. Young Americans focused on such team formation and leadership will be paid a premium for their ability to orchestrate such complexities during the next 20 years. Beyond that, I suspect it will become an expectation for all.

System Integrity - At the turn of this century a lack of integrity emerged in the financial reporting and forecasting of many American companies. The executives responsible for reporting could be incompetent or immoral with no significant consequence to misleading their customers, partners, investors, or regulators. It was a mess, as chronicled following the implosion of the Internet boom in 2001 (think Enron), and the financial industry fiascos preceding the "Great Recession" of 2008/2009. The lack of governance and corporate transparency created "illusions of success" rather than fact-based stories.

America's willingness to correct systemic problems, including accountability for financial reporting, provides a healthier platform than found in most other countries. America has a long way to go, but global money will continue to flow to the U.S., as it is clear that our imperfect governments and markets are well above the fray overseas. After two hundred years of blending a free market economy with a democratic process, our country has produced something far better than dictatorships, monarchies, and tribal systems can show. The capital flowing to America needs to be put to work and invested in ideas and technologies which promise healthy returns to investors. Foreign investment is not the only answer but it is a great wind in the sails of innovative US companies who require youth and vigor.

Power Transformation - Overseas, complex power structures which have existed for thousands of years are being toppled, while tribal systems continue to implode, butchering one another given their simplistic disorder and lack of central structure. Our country is somewhere in-between, evolving through its young life, striking a balance between over-concentration and over-division of power. Our traditional power structures (corporate, government, military, and church) are regularly challenged, tweaked, and then re-tweaked. As with many of the themes in this book, there is great room for improvement, but more to appreciate.

Consider that much of the negative rumbling of any society is fueled by personal economic stress and a lack of hope. That's how Hitler rose to power, fanning the flames of economic discontent in Germany. We don't want to fall prey to such sensationalism during our economic troughs. There's great strength in clarity and direction which comes from a concentrated power structure. I expect a balance will emerge where our leaders will be more effective guiding public policy which benefits most of the people most of the time, not all of the people all of the time, nor some of the people some of the time.

The transformation of traditional power structures in America will provide industrious people with vast new opportunities which were previously inaccessible due to the central control of information, resources and decision making. This is producing an environment ripe for upstarts to innovate and improve.

The balance of power is very complex and very important to our future, as we need certain protections without heavy handed bureaucracy and costly "control". This presents even more opportunity as innovators will develop systems and processes to provide efficient oversight and self-regulating mechanisms to negate top-heavy governance.

A Quickening Pace - Change is certainly constant, but the pace of change is the key distinction from the past. Because of the factors referenced thus far in this chapter, the pace has quickened to a point that legacy processes and lethargic organizations are losing relevance.

The Opportunity? - Focused, adaptable young Americans will see opportunities before most large companies. They'll have no barrier to creating something unique and fitting, given some time, capital and the willingness to take the risk.

"In times of rapid change, experience could be your worst enemy."

... J. Paul Getty

Let's reflect on examples of the newfound accessibility of opportunity for young innovators. Apple did not invent computers or mobile phones, but they improved the user-interface and functionality in ways which made the technology more approachable than their competitors, thus opening vast new markets. Although they are now a mature company, a couple of young Americans started Apple in a garage, like so many other fine American companies. Google, whose founders are immigrants, did not invent Internet search, yet they opened entirely new web applications with their enhanced search sophistication and great simplification of the search experience. Their trajectory in valuation and sector leadership is amazing, becoming the world's largest media company within ten years of their 2004 IPO (Initial Public Stock Offering). Similarly, Facebook did not invent social networking, yet they created accessible functions for broad groups of people to connect, while creating an extendable "platform" which could be used for many purposes beyond the original application.

Breakthrough innovators do not necessarily invent their sector, but must, at a minimum, enhance a sector in a way which offers enough value to enough people to justify investment. Do you believe any of these three companies are sitting still, or do you believe they're seeking new ideas and technologies to help them succeed further? You can look into any one of these companies and see huge war-chests of cash on their balance sheets ready to pay thousands of new employees or purchase hundreds of smaller innovators (you) who bring them great ideas.

The formation of great wealth and the ability of small players to leapfrog the valuations of industrial giants speaks to the changing landscape of innovation and power in America.

Connectivity - Groups naturally help their members in times of need by sharing information, resources or contacts to help their members succeed. This perpetuates the life of the group, by leveraging combined strengths. Whether a wolf pack on a hunt or an enterprising family building multi-generational wealth, it's nice to have friends. Conversely, it stinks for people without such support, historically relegated to the lowest economic and social strata.

Young Americans who leverage tools and technologies to build and nurture personal and professional networks have the potential to surpass the capacity of those who were born into opportunity but remain overly dependent upon the reputation of others. It's another example of changing power structures, facilitated through pervasive communications platforms, group development tools and an appreciation for underdogs winning in America. In a most practical sense, self-starters are attractive to employers, compared with employees who count on their relationships rather than their industriousness. In a perfect world, you build a balance of both.

The Tiger Has Woken - With the newfound awareness of the good life in America and other developed countries, billions of people who did not know a widget existed now want three. Billions of new consumers reside in emerging economies, which were once closed to new ideas. Billions. These people lived through centuries of suppression, misinformation and/or cultural separation but now - like we all would - they want a better life. That means stuff made in America, or manufactured by their local companies using materials and machinery produced in America.

The skyrocketing demand for American ingenuity, education and products will continue to grow as people around the world become more demanding of their suppressive or ineffective governments and as aging accelerates the need for automation and efficiencies. Based on birth trends, some of the world's largest economies (other than the U.S.) will have such a great imbalance of aging they will become highly dependent upon products, services and labor of other countries.

Young Americans who are respectful of the norms and characteristics of other societies, and driven to deliver solutions to unique client segments (on-shore or off-shore) will prosper. Whether one opens a business which caters to a specific global demographic (think local ethnic restaurants), or joins a globally focused company, opportunities will abound.

Big companies don't think about small incremental opportunities, but wait until a sector is defined and proven by the little innovators before acquisitions and consolidations occur. Innovators in America can build relationships with like minded souls in other countries, collectively building access to multiple markets and resource pools. They can do it with no overhead, a low cost of entry, and an investor environment begging for good ideas.

PERSPECTIVE: HOW DO WE COMPARE?

"GDP" (Gross Domestic Product) is a standard economic measure used to analyze and compare the "economic health" of a region or country. To provide context regarding the breadth of the US economy, consider that California's GDP surpasses the GDP of 192 of the world's largest 200 economies. That's right. A single state in our country surpasses all but 8 countries' economic output in the world. Texas' GDP surpasses the combined economies of Argentina, Colombia, Venezuela, Chile, Peru, Ecuador, Guatemala, Uruguay, Panama, Bolivia, Paraguay and El Salvador. The State of Oregon, sitting approximately in the middle of our 50 states' economic output, outpaces 150 of the top 200 economies of countries throughout the world. This demonstrates the power of the US economy and the upside or potential of the emerging markets.

Necessity breeds innovation - Innovation is one of America's greatest strengths, with a long history of absolutely incredible inventions and game-changing enhancements to prior discoveries.

Some innovations occur due to a simple fascination with a challenge or interest, which drives the innovators to obsess to a level others can't comprehend; they find opportunity in the margins. Others innovators are so bored sitting around, they're more inclined to investigate, ponder, and doodle. Sometimes, things have to get so desperate that people rise to the occasion and find solutions which were previously unimaginable. Let's face it, when people are comfortable, they have less incentive to fight for something. But when people are hurting or their prospects are dour, personal and market forces rise up to create new solutions to old problems. Always.

Regardless of what drives you, with many great changes in society, technology, science, entertainment, demographics and academia, you will find more opportunities to innovate than you can imagine. But, you've got to imagine. A young American, doing the same job as 100 middle aged people before them, can see things that the others could not. Maybe youthful energy is the difference, or a fresh set of eyes looking at an old problem, or a hunger for success which elders no longer feel. **Tap it!**

> Mickey Mouse popped out of my mind onto a drawing pad
> on a train ride from Manhattan to Hollywood
> at a time when business fortunes of my brother Roy and myself
> were at lowest ebb and disaster seemed right around the corner.
>
> *... Walt Disney*

There are many opportunities. Our quickly aging population needs help maintaining their independence and has an increasing need for medical care. The US has a weak infrastructure and a financial incapacity to care for elders at the present pace, so what can be done to reduce elders' dependencies while offering efficiencies at the same time? Interestingly, the U.S. is in an enviable demographic position, with many of the top economies in the world saddled with a significantly disproportionate elder population, thus magnifying the opportunity.

Or consider the high cost of a college education and the ridiculous sums of money some people have desperately paid to say they graduated from here or there just to get a job. To fill the growing need for an educated workforce, what can be done to make higher education more accessible to more people without requiring higher taxation or tuition hikes?

How about education in general? With a high school dropout rate of approximately 25%, educators are challenged by a radically different demographic profile, a crumbling parental support structure and a constricting tax funding environment. This complex challenge requires the many good people who are involved in education to repackage it in a form which is relevant and backed by students, parents, teachers, and taxpayers, as if it were a business. Who better to help construct an efficient and relevant educational system than the young Americans who just experienced the ups and downs of the educational system.

Every industry and organization suffers from fits and starts, inefficiencies, product failures and so on. We can wag fingers at what's broken all day long, but that's not the point. Our free market offers incentives to innovators who improve things. It's the American way. Eldercare and education are examples of broad social performance gaps which present great opportunities for innovation. Beyond these, hundreds of other sectors and sub-sectors are waiting for our next generation of leaders to develop and deliver solutions. Tax and investment dollars will flow to people and organizations which improve efficiencies and/or quality of life. New ideas, technologies, and processes will be delivered by people like you, who will profit in the process.

Energized - Over the past 50 years, America's reliance on foreign fuel has compounded our inflation (think cost-of-living), distracted our diplomacy, and created a sense of dependency which concerns many Americans. As the dependency increased, the cost of manufacturing and transportation grew disproportionately and America grew less competitive, exacerbating our trade deficits and job losses.

Americans have been grinding on this dilemma, creating more efficient systems, while reducing some energy use. Hundreds of innovations and opportunities have emerged, while seeding even more through the products and services which support or are fed from the changes.

Those improvements are good but not good enough. The big answer will be economically viable new energy sources which integrate environmentally sustainable practices. Solar and wind initiatives have been increasingly filling gaps and leading to viable alternatives. As certain mechanical and industrial processes depend upon combustion and heat, natural gas has emerged as a potentially profound answer to our country's desire for self-reliance and cleaner energy. The US is on the cusp of bringing vast stores of natural gas to homes and factories across the country. The US may become a net exporter of fuel as it leverages energy sources with innovation.

Because energy is such a large component of US cost structure, from farming, to factories and deliveries, a reduction in such costs will reduce cost of production and thus product/services pricing. This converts to lower cost-of-living for the consumer and lower inflation. This frees money for savings and discretionary spending on things like lattes, cool toys and vacations, perpetually fueling our economy, which is 70% consumer based. This sea change can also translate to consumers overseas who will want American products because of value in addition to the "innovative cool" factor, resulting in the growth of on-shore jobs. The more cost effective products can improve corporate profit margins so companies can plow more money into research and development, funding generations of future innovations.

Wealth distribution - As reported in Deloitte's 2011 study of global wealth composition, American millionaire households are expected to rise from 10.5 million households in 2011 to 20.5 million households in 2020, with wealth growing from $39 trillion in 2011 to $87 trillion in that same timeframe. America is expected to grow its share of global wealth from 42% to 43% in that same period. Most readers are instantly thinking the following:

1) Are there really that many millionaires?
2) How will wealth grow so much, given this lousy economy?
3) Who are these people and how did they do it?

This book's not about the rich and famous, nor suggesting whether you should be one thing or another. You'll learn about the causes-and-effects of personal choices and your ability to establish a solid financial future given the realities around us. The sun always rises, so find a way to survive the occasional dark periods and anticipate the opportunities ahead. Stay focused on what is possible and avoid people and situations which drag you down.

Earning a living is the first financial building block to take advantage of the foundation you have laid with the *You, Inc.* vision. Our next chapter provides the guide and essentials to finding and winning the best jobs, given a challenging environment and your unique brand.

CHAPTER 4
FINDING A JOB

$$$$$$

PAYCHECK $ $ $ $

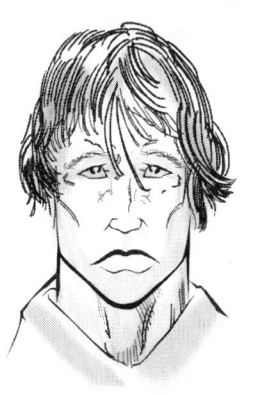

$ $

UNEMPLOYMENT CHECK

$

WELFARE CHECK

Finding A Job

At a certain point in life, dependency is no fun. The pride of earning money is a big source of America's industriousness and resulting strength. That said, many good Americans have made it through tough times thanks to the social services received from government agencies and the compassion of others. Those who feel they're exempt from misfortune are ignorant of the sense of failure that comes with a setback like being let go from a job. You'd be amazed how quickly your confidence disappears when you're terminated, for any reason, in a high unemployment environment.

Over the past 40 years, many Americans have become dependent, comfortable or resigned to simply getting by on the good graces of others. That's got to stop, or our young Americans will be paying more for others' comforts (through taxation) than their own well being. A balance is sorely needed and I expect the U.S. will cut and repackage many social services in the years ahead as our present welfare state is unsustainable.

This anticipated constriction will hurt many dependent families, compounded by the global competitive workplace and respective challenges in finding work. Given this, surely you can see the pain that lies ahead for people who are not in control of their destiny and not positioned to find and keep a job. Becoming a strong earner is the first step to assure that you and your family are rock solid. It's hard to focus on spending money, saving money, or investing money if you have no money!

The rules of job-seeking change as negative economic cycles constrict the traditional stream of opportunities, yet **there are thousands of good companies in America who need you.** The challenge is identifying and connecting with them. This chapter shows you how to multiply your job opportunities and convert them into job offers.

"Kid, do something, even if it's wrong" my father would say as I meandered or was stuck on a decision or task. I hated that expression, as it didn't make sense to me. I was self-righteous and felt a certain clarity of direction was more effective than stumbling forward. After 20 years in the military, a Purple Heart and numerous commendations, my father had learned that life was imperfect and forward progress is critical to solving a problem. He was right.

For most of the past 50 years or so, Americans enjoyed a robust financial environment. Jobs were easier to find, pay rates were growing, and there was a general sense that the party was never going to end. Through such good fortune, it's easy for us to forget the tough times, such as 1982, the year I graduated from college.

Mortgage interest rates hit 17%, compared to 4% in 2013. Just to make it real, that means a $300,000 mortgage required a monthly payment of $4,277, instead of $1,430 per month. This high cost of borrowing paralyzed the people who wanted to buy homes, but could not afford the higher payments. Concurrently, most businesses suffered significant contractions, millions of jobs were lost, industries were leveled, lives were reset, etc. Sound familiar?

I was all dressed up, full of hopes and dreams, looking for a job ... yet nowhere to go except for a neighborhood restaurant. Thank God for that neighborhood restaurant. My buddy Ken was still working his way through college and through his introduction to the manager I took a job as a waiter. I became "almost self-sufficient" while living with my parents, giving me time to land a better job. *Do something.* That next job was not ideal either, but it was my first "professional job". Selling office equipment to businesses was a grind during a time when their capital budgets were limited. A family member had recommended the job saying "if you can make it in that industry, you'll prove that you can do anything". I bit. The average tenure of an office equipment salesperson was six months, before they were fired or determined that the job was extraordinarily difficult. I decided to last one year, and set an income goal for my first full year on the job.

After 15 months on the job, I received a call from a recruiter, working for a national company "seeking proven professionals familiar with the area" to expand their efforts in Portland, Oregon. I've not prepared a resume since, nor sought a job as opportunities have emerged because of my effort, results, rep and a little luck along the way. Whatever it takes, just get started, and be thrilled to get a start.

In spite of the small gripes I could have had about any of my jobs along the way, there were so many things to appreciate beyond compensation. Every job offers an opportunity to learn something new about a company, an industry, other people, new tasks, and most importantly, about yourself. Those experiences are highly portable to the next job, and the next one.

This is no time to be picky, unless you can afford to be. Even then, I'd suggest jumping in with both feet rather than waiting for something special to come along. Look at every job as a step in the right direction, rather than turning down a "lesser job". You're like that beautiful and incredibly expensive jet sitting in a hanger somewhere. Its value drops every day it is not flown, because the industry is changing and innovation keeps going into new jets, discounting yesterday's hot product. The lost time will never be recovered.

Every day is a missed opportunity to grow stronger through new experiences and relationships. Personal growth and increasing financial independence will create momentum which motivate you and perpetuate your success. I believe this is more important than compensation, so I encourage you to pocket your ego and get to work. Do something, even if it's wrong.

LOOKING THROUGH THE EMPLOYER'S EYES

CANDIDATE ESSENTIALS

Having hired and fired employees over the past 30 years, and having trained and studied thousands of people, here's what I've learned to look for in successful new hires:

- **Work ethic.** Will you go above-and-beyond to get the job done, or only perform the bare essentials?
- **Professionalism.** Will you create a positive impression for our company, or will you distract from it?
- **Integrity.** Can I trust you to do the right thing when no one is watching?
- **Teamwork.** Will you be able to balance your personal goals, with those of the team, the clients, and the company?
- **Attitude.** Both positive and negative attitudes are contagious. Will you motivate those around you?
- **Self-managed.** Do you need someone to tell you what to do every day? Can you navigate the speed bumps alone?
- **Dependability.** Doing what you said you'd do in a timely way is a life essential. Can we count on you?
- **Upside.** Business and the environment will change. Do you have the willingness and capacity to learn and adapt?
- **Track Record.** Talk is cheap. What exemplifies these traits in your past?

The Bottom line is that hiring managers seek employees who will provide the lowest risk to their company and who are capable of performing at a reasonably high level with minimal residual problems. Your ability to project this in your interviews and communications will put you at the front of the pack of candidates.

> PERSPECTIVE: THE LITTLE THINGS
>
> On a recent trip to Phoenix, I encountered one of those informal reminders about "what matters" as I was relaxing by the pool prior to a business conference. Nice waitress. Prompt, courteous, friendly. As we chatted ever so briefly and I learned of her 3 years on the job and her anticipated college graduation in the coming months, it became clear that she'll do fine in the job market. She had the essential survival skills to make the most of any job; she'll naturally become stronger. I didn't care where she lived, what kind of car she drove, what her parents did for a living, or even her GPA. I considered her attitude, hustle, and getting through school on her waitress job much more important than other factors. This was someone I'd be glad to interview.

"It's not what you know, but who you know" is another one of the lines I've heard over the years that turned me off. I'd rather focus on the solution, delivering something of great value, not showmanship and glad-handing, right? Yet, having seen so many relationships and business transactions develop over the years, I gained an appreciation for the power of networking and the idea that the best people, the best work, and the best ideas are buried under a mountain of bad stuff which is promoted more effectively.

As a job seeker, you've got to get your story in front of more qualified hiring managers or your potential will be hidden. It would be cool to be magnetic, charismatic, and just wait for the opportunities to line up for you. But, if finding a job or managing your finances were that easy, you wouldn't reading this book, would you? You're not alone.

I've found that people are generally lost in the process of finding work, whether I'm coaching recent graduates looking for their first job or corporate executives between jobs. For most, it goes down as one of the least favorite and highest anxiety experience of their life: the unknown, the high ratio of rejection, and the need to earn a living compounds the pressure. Good news. There's a straight-forward way to get a job and the rough patches along the way are natural experiences which you can minimize. Let's break it down.

PAINT BY NUMBERS

Ok, I'm a process freak. I develop roadmaps for people and organizations to accelerate their success. Through the following phases and steps, job seekers can move forward with a sense of confidence. Following are the steps to take, in the noted order, to optimize your job seeking experience.

THE PREPARATION

1. Define your "Career Objective" in one paragraph.
2. Identify the various jobs which may fit your objective.
3. Define your preferred regions of employment.
4. Determine your minimum acceptable annual compensation, and your realistic "dream compensation" for your 1 year and 5 year horizon. This compensation range provides you - and prospective employers - with a reference point that either works or does not. The sooner you determine that, the quicker you can move onto the right opportunities and effectively focus your energies.
5. Build a resume to capsulate *You, Inc*.
6. Research your preferred region(s) for 20 companies of choice which have the jobs you're interested in. For those companies, determine who is the hiring manager for the job(s) you're interested in, or the best initial contact.

FINDING A JOB   49

7. Identify 5 people you know or want to know, who are connected to the industry of interest, such as recruiters and temp agencies.
8. Review your personal contact directory, including family, friends, teachers, former employers, etc. Take the time to make sure that you have their accurate contact data, including email and phone. Invest your time in building good data.
9. Review online sources for resume submission and "job boards" which are focused on the jobs you're interested in. These resume clearing houses are indexed, searched, and compartmentalized by thousands of hiring managers throughout America. They look for key words and characteristics from millions of resumes, leading to phone and in-person interviews for those who meet their criteria.
10. Contact people who you may list as a reference for a prospective employer; let them know of your next steps in life and ask for their help and permission to provide their name and contact data to prospective employers. Many people miss this step and their references are caught off-guard on the calls or emails they may receive, thus reducing their effectiveness on your behalf. You'll be amazed how much people will advocate for you if you have prepared them and caught them up on your life.
11. Post your "career objective" and the status of your search on your social networking sites, also linking to your resume.
12. Build a spreadsheet, or electronic file of some sort, in which you will list the names, companies, addresses and contact data for the persons identified in steps 6, 7, 8, & 10. You may reference this data over and over, so it is worthwhile to "invest" in building the spreadsheet for efficiency and accuracy.
13. As you begin interviewing with companies of interest, start a separate file you fill with contact data, information about the company, its jobs which are of interest to you and contact history with relevant notes. This structure will help you to keep track of many moving parts, culminating in an informed and confident decision.

THE APPROACH

1. Forward an electronic copy of your resume to your personal network (step 8 above), with a very brief note or letter explicitly stating what's up with you and what you're seeking, along with a copy of your resume. You're not groveling for a job, but informing people of your status, hoping to leverage their contacts and eyes in the market. They're not obligated to reply, right? You're expanding the possibilities, in a way you feel is appropriate.
2. Send brief letters of introduction and a resume to the people in your spreadsheet, as referenced in step 5, 6 & 8 above. Your letter or email note should not be elaborate and your choice of hardcopy/mail, vs. email depends on the ease of getting their necessary contact data. Whatever it takes, get your information in front of these people.
3. Call these people within a couple of days of their receipt (while it is still fresh) and arrange coffee, meetings or phone appointments to discuss their company, the industry, the job search process and their recommendations, etc. Being in front of people is critical in the job hunt. Don't hide behind your text messaging, email, or social networking. While such tools may offer efficiencies, job hunting is a contact sport and you need to connect personally with people. This is a typical "miss" these days.
4. When meeting with these people in initial "exploratory" discussions, document their comments, recommendations or tips on upcoming opportunities. Consider every discussion, email and meeting as a learning opportunity, in addition to an opportunity to update them on your situation and capabilities. Follow-up such meetings with a brief thank you note, while pursuing the leads that may have arisen through them. When I leave a meeting with someone, I expect to have established myself as a trusted resource, who can bring great value to whomever I am introduced.

I want people to advocate for me without doubt. Remember, there are many companies out there who need you, but they don't know who you are. Broadening your visibility, through the leveraging of contacts and strategic communications will greatly enhance the probability of a great connection(s).

5. Concurrently, post your resume to the key online job-boards you identified in step 9 of the Preparation phase.

THE PRESENTATION/INTERVIEW

You began your presentation when you sent the email, included your resume, or had a phone conversation. This is not rocket-science, but as you know, impressions are formed quickly. As you move beyond phone calls and email, the following fundamentals improve the odds of getting to the next step in each job opportunity:

Entry/Receptionist/Admin - Everyone deserves respect. From the second you walked in their door or conversed on the phone with the front-line staff, your tone and clarity demonstrated your character. Assume their opinions matter and they are the gate-keepers to success.

Clothing - If it's an industrial position, a 3 piece suit doesn't fly. If it's an office position, neither do shorts. Try to find the right attire for the zone you're entering. Beyond that, people over-sophisticate the wardrobe process. I'll be much more enamored with the engaging and prepared interviewee who is dressed sharply, but not perfectly, than the well-dressed interviewee who is uptight, unprepared or pretentious. Think balance!

Senses - Body language can instantly solidify or destroy the image you have worked to create. Speech should be clear and articulate, with a volume control that makes the conversation personal and understandable. Both timidity and verbosity usually fail.

Eye contact is a sign of confidence and respect, so show both by looking the interviewer in the eye and not wandering off in the distance during conversation. As you listen, nod as appropriate while you're looking them straight in the eyes and mixing in your smiles with your intensity, deep interest and note taking.

Posture accentuates the feelings candidates have as they often hunch over in a passive/anxious way. When you walk into that meeting, you should "show your thrill" for the opportunity to meet this person, and learn more about their company and the job. You win simply through the experience of being there. Show it.

Intelligent Q&A - Go in prepared with just a few questions you would most like to ask, but wait your turn before you ask them. The interviewer is usually a professional who has done a few more interviews than you have, so it's ok to let them take the lead, rather than trying to demonstrate your leadership. Keep your answers to their questions sharp and to the point, rather than going on-and-on. Every sentence you speak takes time away from other topics which could make a difference. If the time and situation feels right, learn a little bit about the interviewer. You can accomplish your objective of learning more about the company and the person sitting across from you by simply asking "what do you most enjoy about working for XYZ Corp.?"

Pay rate and compensation are near the top of the list for touchy topics. My recommendation is that you learn about the compensation range for the job during the interview, yet avoid cornering the interviewer on the specifics. They may need some space to determine your worth and their ability to thoughtfully right-size the pay may be to your advantage. Also, many first and second interviews occur with professionals who "screen" you prior to your potential meeting with a "hiring manager", who you'll work for and who will determine where you fit within their pay grade for the job.

Pay grades are used to define the minimum, mid-point, and maximum pay for each unique job description. Some smaller employers do this stuff in their heads, but most have a reasonably defined pay range, which keeps them away from HR compliance nightmares for inequitable pay practices.

Instead, focus your questions on the technical, personal and cultural "fit" for you and them. When you find a good employer fit, you can then get down to financial details in your last stage of discussions and reach terms you can both be thrilled with. As you now know, I believe compensation is important, but only a part of the decision process. Money will follow a great alignment of *You, Inc.* with *XYZ, Corp.*

> "Choose a job you love, and you will never have to work a day in your life."
>
> ... *Confucius*

Credentials - Consider that when you leave your interview, another interviewee walks in and attempts to make a solid impression. You've got to use all the tools in your bag to differentiate yourself and create a winning impression. Beyond the basic facts in your resume or the job application, there are personal characteristics you will want to expand upon, to assure your strengths are registered by the interviewer (see earlier "Candidate Essentials"). For these points, be prepared to explain that dimension of yourself, providing examples of how that has helped you and others you have worked with in the past. Themes could include team sports, school projects, work experiences, community service projects, etc. Also, explaining a lesson learned through failure is both honest and humble. Remember that talk is cheap. Demonstrating your proficiencies, characteristics and preparedness for this job is best done through brief stories which bring your words to life.

Credentializing is a very dynamic aspect of interviewing. Many times interviewers will ask questions which are perfect lead-ins for you to make your point, so generally you should capitalize on those windows of opportunity. Or, you may initiate a "story" with the interviewer, as long as the presented strength is something which you feel will be valued by the employer and interviewer. As earlier noted about the importance of avoiding the "me mentality", communicate how your achievement or experience helped teammates, clients, the community, or your employers.

Closing - Rather than leaving the meeting wondering where things go from here, why not ask before you leave? Effectively closing any meeting defines the next steps and gives you a sense of how you did. Sometimes you'll get great clarity and sometimes you won't, but you should always try. For example, "I really enjoyed our talk and appreciate you taking the time to acquaint me with XYZ Corp. What is your timing on making a hiring decision?", or "From our discussion today, I'm very interested in pursuing a career with XYZ Corp. What do you recommend to me so I can build upon today's discussion?", or "I realize your hiring process involves many steps. Before I leave, I'd sure appreciate your opinion of how you feel I would fit into this job and your company."

Follow-up - As always, a simple thank you note or a phone message is a nice touch that can make the difference between two candidates. Control what you can.

Don't Assume - Many people walk out of interviews thinking they did poorly, given that interviews are not in their comfort zone. Relax. Some of the questions you think you fumbled were fumbled by others as well. Interviewers are like poker players; some are big smilers smiling big smiles at all candidates, while others are straight-faced even though they're sold on the candidate. Don't overthink yourself; just do your best and be proud of your effort.

Follow-up Again - You wouldn't assume you lost the job because they didn't call, would you? Some jobs aren't filled as planned, given fluctuating budgets or something as simple as a key leader being on vacation. Also, some selected candidates don't work out. Until you're told the job is filled, your occasional "still interested!" message may make you their first call when they're ready to complete the hire. Use the phone or email, whichever feels most fitting given the individual you're dealing with.

Be a smart loser - We've all lost in life more than we care to admit. Losing intelligently can soften the blow. When you lose a job opportunity - thank them again and ask for their feedback. For example, "May I ask for your guidance? I'm hoping to build on this and become better in my candidacy for my next job opportunity. Is there anything you can recommend to me regarding my communications or my resume?" Another way to leverage your loss to the greatest degree is "Can you recommend another employer in the area who you feel I would be well suited for?" Last, "Might there be another position within XYZ Corp. that you feel would be a good fit for me?" Don't slink away from bad news. Even when you lose, find a way to win.

When you win a job - Celebrate! Be proud and be humbled to have gotten a job and share the news with your network as a courtesy, while thanking anyone involved for their effort and interest. Circling back is a simple touch and a courtesy, a sign of your character, and your brand. *You, Inc.*

When you don't win any job - After you've burned through the first 20 employers from your "Preparatory database", but received no offers, what happens next? If you're like most humans, you'll be bummed out, question your worthiness and think about how you'll respond to stupid redundant questions like "have you found a job yet?".

The likelihood of hitting the ball on your first 20 swings is not high. The pitches are coming fast, you're using new equipment and there are high winds in the ballpark. But you've got to step up to the plate and swing again. Following through on each of the outlined steps, go back and identify 20 more companies and repeat the entire process. Don't throw away files which may provide a future opportunity. Although you're focused on getting a job right now, be strategic and build an arsenal of information and contacts which will help you - or a friend - or a customer - someday. You always win this way, becoming stronger through your experiences and broader network.

RESUME ESSENTIALS

It's just a document, but the science of the resume is to create something which is accurate, relevant and engages the reader.

GENERAL RULES FOR RESUMES:

- **Clarity** - Will readers know what you mean?
- **Brevity** - This is not the interview, but the tool to get the interview. Don't oversell by writing a book. Front and back, two sided on quality paper, with additional pages should job history warrant.
- **Key words** - The art of the resume is using words which are engaging, not flowery, but balanced with precision.
- **Accuracy** - This is a first impression of you. Get it right.
- **Structure** - Employers will not read your resume if it is not somewhat standardized. There are ways to make a resume "you", but be careful about "cute or different".

STRUCTURAL STANDARDS FOR RESUMES:

- Contact data at top. Make it easy for people to reach you.
- Your Name and "Resume" top and center.
- Objective: next lower top and center; avoid being overly specific, while also avoiding overly broad.
- Job history: date range of employment, company, position(s) and a very brief outline of what you did or accomplished or learned at that job.
- Skills listing: columnar format works well, as simple listings suffice, such as "MS Office", "Database Administration", or "Client Service". Focus to those skills most applicable in the industry of interest. Less is better.
- Education: list year graduated, degree/level of education, school name, any particular areas of focus.
- Personal Interests: Skiing, Travel, etc.
- Accomplishments: recognition or awards you received should be profiled if they support your brand.

FORMATTING RESUMES:

- Avoid busy fonts, use 11-12 point for body, bold for titles, and 14-16 for major headings.
- If you do not have an eye for layout, use a resume service, or hire a friend and spend your money on another young American who specializes in such work.
- Create an electronic copy of the document, using your word processing tool of choice and file format others can open, or a PDF file which retains your document structure regardless of the reader's technology. This provides a small file which can be routed electronically (think viral), along with your cover letter or email introductory note. Do not secure the document as that may limit automated resume scans used by many employers and recruiters.

> ### PERSPECTIVE: REFERENCES ARE GOLDEN
>
> One of the greatest challenges for employers is determining which candidates are real and which ones are "acting real". Many awesome candidates have turned into employers' worst nightmares. When an interviewer is "almost" hooked on you, but questions naturally remain regarding your ability or character, references help you close the deal. In other cases, interviewers want to hire you, but need to affirm their assessment through discussions and verifications with your references. In most cases, their HR policy requires this.
>
> Have reference data readily available to provide as opportunities mature. If you feel particularly good about an opportunity, give them your references on a separate sheet of paper at the end of the interview, or in a thank you note following the interview. Reduce the employer's verification effort by providing an accurate reference listing; name, company, title, address, phone and email, along with a notation of their relationship with you.

EMPLOYMENT SOURCES - DEMYSTIFIED

Identifying Employers - Given the task outlined in the preparatory steps earlier in this chapter, you need to identify prospective employers. There is a great deal of information available to those willing to sleuth employer data out and be thoughtful in their preparation. I recommend using local business directories, industry and business award listings, web-search, trade associations, acquaintances in the industry, etc. I would leverage all of these resources at the same time in order to rapidly broaden my pool of possibilities.

Recruiters - "Headhunters" usually earn a fee based on their success placing you with an employer and often tied to the longevity of your employment. As their clients hire more people in the years ahead, recruiters will naturally receive more opportunities for placements if the clients are thrilled with the candidates the recruiter presented and "placed" earlier at their company. Will you make the recruiter look good? Treat the recruiter as you would an employer, being prompt, professional, and ready to go. They can also offer some coaching, given their relationship with the employer and their laps around the job search track. By developing a strong trust with the recruiter, they will work harder for you and put you in front of more qualified opportunities. As you may engage recruiters, I encourage you to first determine their experience dealing with your field of interest and assure that they're "employer paid", not "employee paid". The last thing you need is a bill to pay, right?

Networking groups - On your own, the job hunt can drag you down and it's tough to cover a lot of ground in a big city. Consider the resources of focused groups of people sharing a common objective or dilemma (i.e. young unemployed people). Effectively arranged, they can broaden members' horizons and offer emotional support given the shared interest and/or challenge. You might create your own group (you, the master networker!) by inviting people who are also looking for work, but who have complimentary, non-competitive job interests. It's amazing when a small group of people pull together, using their collective eyes, ears, minds and personal networks. It's the new order. Leverage it!

Temp Agencies - Once considered the last resort and stigmatized by the image of a secretarial pool, temp agencies have emerged as a viable source for candidates seeking entry points to future jobs. Employers have increased their use of temp agencies to augment their regular staffing and strategic outsourcing. As employers' regulatory burdens, bad hire expenses, and litigation has increased over the past few decades, they see temp agencies as a good way to test new employees, thus lowering risk.

A temp agency is like a recruiter and you should mirror the concepts recommended in the earlier section. Additionally, consider in advance whether you're interested in a pure temp position which is often short term in nature, a contract position for a designated range of time, or whether you seek strictly "temp to hire", meaning they plan to move the position to employee status if you work out over a designated period.

Contract/Freelancing - Many young Americans are shedding traditional jobs to work for multiple clients rather than a single employer. This works well if you have strong skills which companies do not staff in-house; they can put your skills to work without having to add you to their long-term payroll. Freelancing can offer you a bridge to longer term employment, paying the bills along the way, or in addition to a primary job to grow income on the side. For others, it's their career choice.

Be aware that if you're a contractor/freelancer, your benefits and "employer taxes" are not paid by an employer; you're responsible for insurance and certain tax duties (i.e. paying employer taxes). As you'll see in the coming "Jeopardy" chapter, taxes are not to be toyed with.

For this book, I hired 4 freelancers to help me (Artist, Graphics Artist, Book Layout Specialist, and Editor) and 2 companies (Printer and Distributor). They're great at what they do and helped me to bring this book to you in a cost-effective and timely way, enhancing its quality. They choose whether to work from home or an office, are not accountable to me for their hours worked or the time of the day they start or finish. They are comfortable talking on the phone, balanced with good written skills. They adapt as needed to establish personal connections, yet in an efficient way.

Although I look forward to possibly meeting them someday, all communications have been through email or phone. They can choose to work with me again, or not, and vise-versa with no sense of obligation. They could work as employees for companies but for varied reasons choose freelancing. I'm glad they did.

Entrepreneurship - Building and running a company is a big step-up from freelancing. Another self-employed alternative to traditional employment, entrepreneurs are significant creators of jobs and wealth in the US. The key decision point for anyone considering building a business is the sheer effort to set the business up, handle administration, accounting, sales, service, and product development ... and repeat this every day. This presents a steep learning curve for someone not already intimate with some or all of these functional areas. I was actually educated in the School of Entrepreneurism at Oregon State University and was scared off from starting a business, as the daunting odds of success became apparent. That's why most people join a company, to focus on fewer tasks and learn while being paid. I have deep respect for the millions of entrepreneurs who take risks and make the effort every day. They're a cornerstone of America's economic success.

Back to reality, the failure rate for new businesses is quite high, with conservative estimates showing 25% of new businesses failing within one year and 50% within 5 years. Many entrepreneurs have the "right stuff", but their interesting concepts never get off the ground. A lack of market alignment, sheer effort, financial support and good old fashioned luck play into the success and failure rates of new businesses. Maybe you've got enough of the right stuff to give it a go? I was chicken and chose the employment route.

OTHER EMPLOYMENT CONCEPTS

Employer Sizes - Larger entities offer greater opportunities to progress through various jobs, as they naturally have more jobs and job classifications than smaller employers. Conversely, smaller companies may not offer such formal opportunities to advance, yet employees are often introduced to cross-functional duties as part of their standard job, given the lack of scale in a small company.

So, if you like highly focused jobs with functional and geographic upside, the larger entity is a good play, with smaller entities often offering a diverse but limited experience right out of the gates. Employee benefits, such as healthcare and retirement savings plans, are generally much more robust with a larger employer, typically beyond 25 employees. Of course, there are exceptions and as with all concepts, this will evolve. Until then, unless you work for an employer who offers strong benefits and savings plans, you'll need to address these important items on your own.

Jobs for Life - In years past, people usually aspired to work for a single employer their whole life, due to fewer employers, a slower business pace, and a less complex economic landscape. What was once a matter of honor and loyalty eroded with economic realities and increasing mobility. The single employer vision is an outmoded and unrealistic objective for most of us. My guess is that you did not list "work for a single employer" anywhere in your *You Inc.* vision document. Loyalty is very cool and I'm a big believer in sticking with something, but there's a balance we need to find with our practical needs.

My strong encouragement is that you assess each prospective employer for their potential to help you reach your initial and mid-term goals. Be realistic about business cycles and the bumps-and-bruises which are natural for all industries, often resulting in different opportunities than participants had anticipated. Put your heart into every job "just because", with the idea that you'll never be ashamed of your effort even when things don't work perfectly for you in the end. From there, worst case, you're positioned nicely for the next stepping stone in your career and can stand proud - always - for the work that you did.

Others skate to the puck,
I skate to where the puck will be.

... Wayne Gretzky

My career with Automatic Data Processing (ADP) began when ADP's recruiter mailed me that month's Forbes Magazine with a cover story profiling ADP's position in the market, their unparalleled financial consistency, and their stellar reputation. Yet, I didn't understand how a computer services company could succeed, when mini-computers were storming onto the business scene (PCs had not been invented yet). Before accepting their job offer, I went to the bookstore and picked up a copy of John Naisbitt's MegaTrends, which highlighted ten major trends which he believed would reshape America. Three of them involved information management and I extrapolated the effects on ADP and ADP's effects upon the business world.

I'm glad to have leveraged an industry trend for my career choice before outsourcing was even a word. By the time I left ADP 15 years later, 1,367 corporations had agreed to outsource portions of their computer operations with ADP, through my consulting and sales.

Comparative analysis - It's good to have sense for the compensation ranges and trends of different jobs. As referenced in chapter 2, certain jobs are more likely to be eliminated or hyper-competitive than others. You'll find it advantageous to identify an industry which has a strong future, while also considering an industry that interests you. As that industry or your interest shifts, you can reassess and reposition accordingly. Remember, job choices are not make-or-break life decisions, but are certainly important enough to warrant thoughtful and strategic planning.

On the next two pages, you'll find a sampling of jobs, their current average annual pay, and their anticipated growth rates from 2010 - 2020, compliments of the Bureau of Labor Statistics. While you do not want to choose a career path completely on income and job growth, those two items are important considerations, alongside your skills and preferences.

Occupations with the largest growth in jobs **percentage**

Job Title	2010 Median Wage	2010 Number Of Jobs	2010 - 2020 Growth New Jobs	Rate
Personal care aides	$ 19,640	861,000	607,000	**71%**
Home health aides	$ 20,560	1,017,700	706,300	**69%**
Biomedical engineers	$ 81,540	15,700	9,700	**62%**
Helpers—stonemasons	$ 27,780	29,400	17,600	**60%**
Helpers—carpenters	$ 25,760	46,500	25,900	**56%**
Veterinary techs	$ 29,710	80,200	41,700	**52%**
Reinforcing iron workers	$ 38,430	19,100	9,300	**49%**
Physical therapist assistants	$ 49,690	67,400	30,800	**46%**
Helpers—pipe & plumbing	$ 26,740	57,900	26,300	**45%**
Meeting & event planners	$ 45,260	71,600	31,300	**44%**
Medical sonographers	$ 64,380	53,700	23,400	**44%**
Occupational therapy assistants	$ 51,010	28,500	12,300	**43%**
Physical therapist aides	$ 23,680	47,000	20,300	**43%**
Glaziers	$ 36,640	41,900	17,700	**42%**
Interpreters and translators	$ 43,300	58,400	24,600	**42%**
Medical secretaries	$ 30,530	508,700	210,200	**41%**
Marketing research & specialists	$ 60,570	282,700	116,600	**41%**
Marriage & family therapists	$ 45,720	36,000	14,800	**41%**
Brickmasons & blockmasons	$ 46,930	89,200	36,100	**41%**
Physical therapists	$ 76,310	198,600	77,400	**39%**
Dental hygienists	$ 68,250	181,800	68,500	**38%**
Bicycle repairers	$ 23,660	9,900	3,700	**38%**
Audiologists	$ 66,660	13,000	4,800	**37%**
Health educators	$ 45,830	63,400	23,200	**37%**
Stonemasons	$ 37,180	15,600	5,700	**37%**
Cost estimators	$ 57,860	185,400	67,500	**36%**
Medical scientists	$ 76,700	100,000	36,400	**36%**
Mental health counselors	$ 38,150	120,300	43,600	**36%**
Pile-driver operators	$ 47,860	4,100	1,500	**36%**
Veterinarians	$ 82,040	61,400	22,000	**36%**

DATA SOURCE: U.S. Bureau of Labor Statistics (Job titles shortened for brevity)

Occupations with the largest growth in job count

Job Title	2010 Median Wage	2010 Number Of Jobs	2010 - 2020 Growth Rate	2010 - 2020 New Jobs
Registered nurses	$ 64,690	2,737,400	26%	711,900
Retail salespersons	$ 20,670	4,261,600	17%	706,800
Home health aides	$ 20,560	1,017,700	69%	706,300
Personal care aides	$ 19,640	861,000	71%	607,000
Office clerks, general	$ 26,610	2,950,700	17%	489,500
Food prep & servers	$ 17,950	2,682,100	15%	398,000
Customer service reps	$ 30,460	2,187,300	16%	338,400
Heavy & tractor-trailer drivers	$ 37,770	1,604,800	21%	330,100
Laborers, freight, stock movers	$ 23,460	2,068,200	15%	319,100
Postsecondary teachers	$ 45,690	1,756,000	17%	305,700
Nursing aides & orderlies	$ 24,010	1,505,300	20%	302,000
Childcare workers	$ 19,300	1,282,300	20%	262,000
Bookkpg & Accnting clerks	$ 34,030	1,898,300	14%	259,000
Cashiers	$ 18,500	3,362,600	7%	250,200
Elementary school teacher	$ 51,660	1,476,500	17%	248,800
Receptionists & clerks	$ 25,240	1,048,500	24%	248,500
Janitors & cleaners	$ 22,210	2,310,400	11%	246,400
Landscaping/Groundskeeping	$ 23,400	1,151,500	21%	240,800
Sales representatives	$ 52,440	1,430,000	16%	223,400
Construction laborers	$ 29,280	998,800	21%	212,400
Medical secretaries	$ 30,530	508,700	41%	210,200
Supervisors of office & admin	$ 47,460	1,424,400	14%	203,400
Carpenters	$ 39,530	1,001,700	20%	196,000
Waiters and waitresses	$ 18,330	2,260,300	9%	195,900
Security guards	$ 23,920	1,035,700	19%	195,000
Teacher assistants	$ 23,220	1,288,300	15%	191,100
Accountants & auditors	$ 61,690	1,216,900	16%	190,700
Licensed Nurses	$ 40,380	752,300	22%	168,500
Physicians & surgeons	$ 111,570	691,000	24%	168,300
Medical assistants	$ 28,860	527,600	31%	162,900

DATA SOURCE: U.S. Bureau of Labor Statistics (Job titles shortened for brevity.)

Work is the critical beginning of financial independence. Any job is a step in the right direction and once employed, you'll want to dig deep and build upon what got you the job in the first place. Our next chapter, "Protecting Your Job", identifies the many ways you can build your career and become a great resource to anyone you work with.

CHAPTER 5

PROTECTING YOUR JOB

Protecting Your Job

*It's a recession when your neighbor loses his job;
it's a depression when you lose your own.*

... Harry S. Truman

While getting hired is a really great accomplishment, building upon that and **staying hired** is crucial. Work disruption can be catastrophic, as pay stoppage will quickly purge your savings and <u>rock your ego</u>. Yet job-protecting skills are counter intuitive and contrary to what we have learned through educational, social and media influences.

A recurring theme in this book is that the rules of engagement have changed. Because of the economic factors noted earlier, you can assume that your job is scrutinized at all times. That others want your job. Your job is subject to consolidation, revision, or elimination. This has become increasingly prevalent over the past twenty years. There are ways to avoid the inherent insecurity of worrying that your jobs and financial future is predicated on the whim of some person somewhere making some decision we had no influence upon.

The Webster Dictionary defines indispensable as someone "not subject to being set aside or neglected" and "absolutely necessary". The defensive posture on this chapter's cover reflects the feelings of many American employees, as they protect their job by fighting off others. The best path is quite opposite. This chapter is all about building on your brand to effectively integrate into a workplace, while developing capabilities which will endear you to your employer, clients, teammates, and prospective employers.

A CAST OF CHARACTERS

Do you ever play games involving varied character roles? I've played just enough chess to know I suck at chess, yet the pecking order of the players adds a game within the game, which fascinates me.

Pawns are dispensable. Without regret they become collateral damage in the effort to win the overall game. Pawns don't get asked their opinion, but are moved forward at great risk to the pawn but little risk to the gamer. For the benefit of the important characters protected at the back of the board, pawns provide a low-cost front-line, simply marching forward whether they like it or not. Other pieces on the game board are increasingly indispensable as their abilities increase to adapt, change directions, or respond to a changing competitive landscape.

The queen is the opposite of the pawn, with universal directional options, no distance limitations, and protection provided by other pieces given the premium the gamer places on her power. The many other chess pieces have capabilities between the lowly pawn and the all powerful queen, as you'll find in most workplaces.

In fact, employers don't want a bunch of Queens. Instead, they seek a cast of characters with a wide range of talents and personalities who will work together in a complimentary fashion to help their organization win their game. These organizations use many pawns (although they're increasingly outsourced) to handle menial tasks. It is important that you determine where you want to reside on the pawn and queen spectrum.

As you choose your path, there are specific skills and characteristics you can develop which will make you indispensable to your present employer and a desirable future candidate to the world.

<u>INITIAL</u> ON THE JOB ESSENTIALS

The "Candidate Essentials" I referenced in the last chapter are still relevant. Hopefully, through your emphasis of such strengths in your interview process, you won the job and now have the opportunity to prove the hiring manager was right in selecting you. Review that listing and know that the balance of this chapter augments those points.

Dependability - Arriving at work on-time, following through on tasks you're responsible for and being consistent in your approach makes you "dependable" in the eyes of an employer. Many good employees do not attain dependable status because ... because of this ... because of that. After the first few excuses, they might as well tell people the dog ate their homework. While workmates smile and nod as the stories unfold, the excuses are creating a lasting impression.

Work Ethic - Do you complete just enough work to meet requirements, or do you occasionally go above and beyond to deliver something of greater value than expected by your employer and clients? Life's imperfect and many challenging situations arise which require extra effort. Find a way to give that extra effort from time-to-time, rather than doing just enough.

Tasks In The Margins - Job descriptions and leaders' directions only go so far. There are tasks which could be construed as someone else's responsibility, or no one's responsibility, but a missing link which must be connected to the balance of your company's solution. Will you jump in, without trumpeting your hero status and complete what needs to be done?

Expertise & Quality - Part of America's business strength comes from its determination to learn what works or doesn't, and how to correct products and processes as needed. Quality control is a broad organizational discipline, which is required in these days of instantaneous market feedback. Are you committed to being an expert at your job and constantly focused on how you and your teammates can efficiently deliver the best solution to clients?

"Pleasure in the job puts perfection in the work."

... Aristotle

Utility - Your role in your company is part of a larger "supply chain" which comes together to deliver an end product to a customer. There are many interdependencies and the best people understand them well enough to identify when one dimension or another has broken down. Through this broader vision, employees doing one job can more effectively communicate a need to a responsible teammate or plug into another job to fill the gap. Are you learning how your job correlates with others in your workplace and how your products and services are connected to other dimensions in the industry?

Collaboration - Many high school and university curriculums are beginning to emphasize teamwork as a life skill. Yet, many American workers still see themselves as soloists or lack the needed skills to collaborate effectively. Also, your company's leaders may give head fakes to employees, with their chatter about teamwork, right alongside individual performance targets. What gives?

A balance (there's that word again) is required, where you perform as expected or better in your core duties, while constantly making the effort to help the team, however your manager defines the team. If you can constantly rise above the daily focus of your job, and make every effort to help others around you for the common good, you'll be pleased with yourself and will have pleased others as well.

The ability to contribute to the collective success of a group will empower you, protecting your present role and positioning you for future opportunities.

Get Ahead, Get Along - There are many complexities to the interpersonal and social fabric of an effective workplace. Here are the three I believe most worthy of focus:

- **Cliques** - In the workplace, it's great to build friendships, but not when those friendships become overly insular and/or your decisions within the workplace are overly influenced by them. Cliques disallow the engagement of new participants and by nature present risk to the employer and its employees. Reach out beyond your comfort zone to engage others socially and intellectually. You'll be better for it, and so will they.
- **Pettiness** - We've all endured endless reality TV, sensationalist headlines and social networking's microscoping of others' lives; such pettiness is now prevalent in most group environments. I've seen an unhealthy increase in put-downs, conversations about others and siding with people on topics which aren't relevant to the business at hand. Also, when your co-workers fail, rather than calling them out, maybe you cut them some slack and hold off reacting until you see a recurring pattern. Then, talk with them, or your manager in seeking a constructive solution or backing off altogether. There is no place for pettiness on a team.
- **Diversity** - Another incredible American strength is our diversity and protections for such diversity in workplaces and communities. We've come a long way since our country's founding, with the fits and starts that occur with any major social transformation. But we still have work to do.

I was born in Taipei, Taiwan during my father's military service, then lived in Turkey and Germany, before settling in Oregon as my father completed his military career in Vietnam. It wasn't until

I came to America that I experienced racism, having grown up alongside kids of all colors on the very integrated military bases. Color is only one form of diversity, but representative of many other differences in our society. Our next generation (you) is so much smarter about this topic than past generations that I could just stop here, but I won't.

Our economic security will be greatly enhanced by capitalizing on the collective efforts and insights of all of our people. As a young American, you can enhance your career through inclusion and a conscious commitment to disallow alienation of people based upon some personal characteristic which has nothing to do with the job at hand.

Have Some Fun - With all this talk of "improvement" and "competition" and "process" it's easy to forget what we're all striving for, which is essentially quality of life. Most of us don't relish spending 35% of our day in a sterile workplace. I'm telling you right now that in even the most difficult work environments, people can have a lot of fun. Some of my favorite memories come from activities, stupid jokes, and the goofiness that just happens when you put a bunch of people together in the workplace stewpot. Be open to laugh, to share a funny story and loosen up a bit. Take your breaks, get away from your desk at lunch. It will do everyone some good. Beyond that, go home, turn work off, and enjoy the fruits of your labor.

> "When he worked, he really worked.
> But when he played, he really PLAYED."
>
> ... Dr. Seuss

ADVANCED ON THE JOB ESSENTIALS

"There is nothing more difficult to carry out,
nor more doubtful of success,
nor more dangerous to handle,
than to initiate a new order of things."

... *Niccolo Machiavelli*

Constructive disruption - Remember, as a new hire, you're the fresh set of eyes and ears in a company and can help identify "new and improved" opportunities. However, occasionally new employees want to change the world a bit too soon, and a bit too much in their employer's and peers' opinions. Even if you think you have awesome ideas when you move into a new job, hold back a bit. By nature, group dynamics disallow outsiders coming in and reshaping things, unless things are in significant disrepair and the incoming employee is a well regarded figurehead. As a new and less experienced employee, you're better off to humbly absorb your new job duties, consistently master them, and as your relationships mature within the workgroup, you'll identify people who are genuine sounding boards.

Your leaders and mature teammates have seen plenty of young heroes march in with their grand ideas and big talk, without the focus and commitment to do their job. Instead, place 95% of your focus on mastery and performance for your given job, with the balance of your time spent on creative improvements. Within that framework, you can begin to constructively disrupt, introducing your ideas for product and process improvement to the appropriate teammates and/or leadership in a thoughtful and credible manner. Avoid overly righteous positions, instead vet your theories with a range of people in order to evolve the idea to a better state. This process assimilates others into your ideas, which is critical in effectively implementing change in a workplace or industry.

One of the tools I have used over the years is a simple notepad which I pull out whenever I am struck by an idea or concept. I categorize the ideas, rank them for impact compared to effort, get others' perspectives, then determine the "ROI" (Return On Investment) for my time and the company's attention. Ultimately, I do not want to introduce a prospective "improvement" until I clearly believe in it myself. From there, I can march confidently forward. As of today's writing, my idea pad is 5 pages deep, with 32 interesting concepts I am presently pondering.

Perspective: Solutions

Early in my career, I reported to a "Chris B." in Chicago. Frustrated one day by something I felt was ineffective in our company, I explained my frustration and vented a bit to Chris. He listened intently, nodded, then offered his view. "Paul, I'm a busy guy. I hear you on this one, but I don't need more problems. You're a smart guy. The next time you bring me a problem, I want you to also bring me solutions to that problem."

I've been really fortunate to work for great leaders like Chris throughout my professional life. They cut to the chase with their honesty, while giving me plenty of runway to bring new ideas to the table, occasionally taking risks on my behalf because they believed in me. Their sponsorship kept me engaged in the bigger mission because I felt I could affect things in a positive way, *beyond my job description*. I didn't need a promotion, nor additional compensation, but relished the belief that my passion to innovate could be leveraged.

Avoiding Dilution - Multi-tasking is a powerful capability which allows people to perform many functions at one time. In years past, this was a description reserved for very special individuals who could achieve more in the same amount of time as their peers who lacked that mental juggling skill. New technologies have emerged, allowing most adults to concurrently host multiple conversations, using email, text messaging, phone and face-to-face conversations. Different people, different topics, different devices, different mediums, all at the same time. Very, very cool. Kinda.

Once we get past being enamored with the sizzle of the technologies and enabling applications, the effect of such concurrency is dilution in quality and a lack of attention to detail. In addition to this dilution, there is a negative effect of engaging in superficial interpersonal communications. These are the reasons to reduce multi-tasking.

As a very early adopter of performance enhancing technologies and an advocate for personal productivity, I'll be the last to rain on the parade of "cool tools". Balance is needed, using these tools to enhance your communications in more meaningful ways. Looking back, I realize that when I was in conversation with someone and a call or text came in, glancing at my phone was bad form. When you're at the counter placing your order for coffee, are you on the phone at the same time? Or when you're walking between things are you heads-down texting? If so, you're missing some really important dimensions to life, common courtesies and opportunities which you'll never know existed.

Efficiencies aside, in the years ahead, the people who behave like machines will be treated like machines.

The Asses You'll Meet Along the way - People who derive their power from intimidation and put-downs are poor souls who are typically driven by their deep insecurities rather than some sort of innate hatred of people. Whether such people are bosses or co-workers, they lurk in many groups, ruining the days of good people. This book doesn't solve world hunger nor will it eradicate such people from your life. Given that, how do you excel when you find yourself in such a situation at work?

When you perform as outlined throughout this chapter, you naturally repel intimidation as your value and confidence grow. In time, asses will be "found out" as sediment sinks to the bottom, but if the problem persists beyond a year or so, you should plan to move on. You're building a brand which will define its preferred terms someday, although you may have to suck it up and bite your lip as you honor the ass who is your teammate or commanding the ship ("get ahead, get along"). If you so love the job and want badly to remain with the company - on your terms - you can engage your HR representative or trusted supervisor to discuss a possible remedy. Because I perform my job at a high level I don't have to work for asses. If you do the right stuff, you won't either.

What's Your EQ? - For many years, intelligence ("IQ") was a primary indicator of employment performance, with little attention given to the emotional quotient ("EQ"). Fortunately, both are now recognized as important characteristics of the best employees, given the proven dysfunction that occurs when the business mission is derailed through private matters and interpersonal conflict.

Family, financial, workplace, spiritual, physical and social parts of your life are all ebbing and flowing in your psyche throughout your average day. Just as your friends will not want to discuss the minutia of your job over beverages, your personal concerns generally don't deserve emphasis at work. I encourage you to build the skills to compartmentalize each dimension of your life in order to maintain focus on your day job. There will be many opportunities to weave your personal life into work, and share parts of your life with trusted teammates.

The best gauge on such matters is to constantly assess your conversations and actions and adjust accordingly:

- How interesting is this to someone else?
- How relevant is this to someone else?
- Is this a positive or negative topic?
- Is this a one-way or two-way conversation?
- Is this affecting my performance or attention to the job?

Another dimension of EQ is your ability to handle set-backs and dysfunctional personalities or groups in the workplace. Do you have the discipline to avoid overreaction to disappointments? Are you the calming influence on the team, encouraging people to step back and consider others' views, or are you someone who fans the flames of discontent in order to fit in? Using your mouth half as much as your ears, you will be much more effective in a work group.

"Make your work to be in keeping with your purpose"

... Leonardo da Vinci

Walking the Talk - Most people are left or right brain dominant, either oriented to doing a task or talking about a task. A small proportion can do both, but this is something many should aspire to. The world is full of talk and vision but quite short on those who can implement their vision. You will do well to build a rep for bringing ideas to the table, backed by your actions and results, balanced with collaboration.

Build Out Your Network - In the last chapter, I encouraged joining or creating a job search networking group... Morph that concept by developing a broader network which can help you throughout your career:

- **Industry professionals** who do not compete with you, but share the same interests, will value your common ground and the ability to share information, which can help each participant win in their respective games.
- **Mentors** will recognize your initiative and be willing to share their perspectives from time to time. Although this may simply be an occasional breakfast or beverage, accomplished professionals are generally glad to help rookies, as most received help on their journey.
- **Community organizations** allow you to use your skills to support an initiative you care about, while building experiences in a very different environment. You'll find yourself surrounded by like minded people, along with very wise and talented leaders who gravitate to such social causes.

Note: Reciprocity is a key ingredient in the networking ecosystem, as strong players become disenchanted with the imbalance from pure takers. As you select and align with networks, remember the essential need to feed the network; people who are contributing are much more likely to get help. Membership in more than a couple of groups will stretch your capacity to give.

Always Growing - Professionals grow through time on the job as they're regularly presented with new workplace variations, however growth can be most fruitful with the addition of strategic education. Some companies do a nice job helping their employees develop, but such development is often limited to in-house skills and lacks 360 degree career planning. It's really up to you. I recommend that you take the initiative to lead this process, with an annual review of your plan, establishing the next year's curriculum roadmap. As you review your

1 year vs. 5 year plan, what skill or educational gaps could you fill in order to reach the next level in your career progression?

Conferences, workshops, on-line courses and college curriculum are examples of turnkey tools which exist in the market to make you stronger and help *You, Inc.* evolve. Education also fills the time for a young American whose budget may not allow for as many entertainment and social activities. Each time you develop a new skill, your confidence grows as does your enthusiasm. This justifies your investment and increases the value of *You, Inc.*

> "Success usually comes to those
> who are too busy to be looking for it"
>
> ... Henry David Thoreau

The Prima Donna - If you adopt many of these strategies to be successful in the workplace, you're going to be proud of yourself and want people to know that you rock. You've got to avoid that temptation, masking your accomplishments and vigor just a bit. How you carry yourself can make a big difference in your workplace relations and effectiveness. There are many geniuses throughout history who were ineffective because they cultivated an image of greatness rather than service or conformity. On one hand, you want to constantly improve yourself and be a high performer, but on the other you need to respect the EQ of your teammates and the realities of group dynamics.

Better to avoid hyping your accomplishments and incredibly wonderful life if it de-motivates or significantly distances you from the pack. An odd thing I learned along the way is that the higher you fly, while earning respect from many, you earn just as much resentment from others. This is a sad truth of human nature, given the average human's anxieties, jealousies or lack of ambition. Don't hide your accomplishments, but err on the side of humility rather than trumpeting everything to your peers. In time, you will naturally gain the appropriate respect.

Contrary to bragging, I encourage you to document and review your accomplishments and developments with your boss periodically. This will insure that they understand the effort you are making and the value you are building. They can provide feedback, guidance, and will be more inclined to consider such progress in future promotions, wage assessment, and the support for future reference requests.

"Late in life I learned that the next best thing to doing really great work was reminding people that I'd done really great work".

... John Rockefeller

Self Starter - Beyond initial instructions, do you need a leader to tell you what to do and when to do it? Do you need to know all before you can start a job or project? Self starters figure out the way to accomplish objectives, within the logical boundaries of a company and work environment and without requiring constant oversight. It would be nice to be considered by a leader when they're seeking someone to tackle a problem, right?

I encourage you to strive to become a go-to resource within your workplace. You can do so by making the effort to figure things out, keeping your superiors informed without it appearing self-promotional, while always making the effort to include and acknowledge others in your development of solutions.

"Imagination is more important than knowledge"

... Einstein

Is It Time To Go? - Job mobility is a very positive dimension of capitalism, as resources such as labor redistribute given the ebb and flow of supply and demand. If you lack the skills or connectivity to make a job work, usually your employer's doing you a favor by firing you, or you by firing them. There is an assumed "better fit" with another employer or your replacement employee and the upgrade raises the game for all involved.

When you feel it's time to go, I encourage you to look in the mirror and question yourself before you launch into this transition:

- Have you done what you can do to optimize the existing job?
- Have you engaged in an honest discussion about your aspirations with your superior or another company leader to determine if other opportunities exist elsewhere in the company?
- Are you sure that the grass will be greener somewhere else?

As mentioned earlier, I've had all sorts of concerns and frustrations with jobs throughout my life. What I learned by sticking with my two primary employers (15 years and 10 years as of this writing) is that I grew significantly after the 3rd year in the job. Even after many incredible experiences and a few successes early in adulthood, my effectiveness mushroomed by hanging in there through the ups-and-downs which are natural to all organizations. Job hopping disallows "mastery", which only occurs after years in a job or company. I'm not suggesting you retain an employer for life, but get the most out of each situation and attempt to experience the great feelings that come from building expertise.

> "Many of life's failures are people who did not realize how close they were to success when they gave up."
>
> ... *Thomas A. Edison*

When It's Time To Go - Once you've reached the point of no return and decide to change employers, I encourage you to do it right:

- **Define your new terms** - With your job experience, you have a better understanding of your desired compensation range, and the improvements you seek in the next job. Maybe it's just the opportunity to explore a different industry or area. Write this out to guide you in evaluating new job opportunities.

- **Review the chapter "Finding A Job"** - Although you're wiser from your recent job experience, those concepts will apply every time you ponder a job change. Maximize your compensation and/or job fit by attending to the details and checklists, including revising your resume to your liking.
- **Be discreet** - unless you have a very tight relationship with your superior, do your exploration privately. Employers discount employees who lack a long term commitment. Private discussions with co-workers becomes office gossip quickly.
- **Land a job before you quit** - It doesn't feel fair, but without a job, your credibility drops with prospective employers. For that reason, and your likely need for cash flow, if at all possible don't jump until you're set with your new gig.
- **Consider "Total Compensation"** - As you know, compensation goes well beyond the paycheck. Does your prospective new employer offer more or less 401k/savings match, healthcare insurance, parking, educational reimbursement, etc.
- **Tighten Up Your Messaging** - Your reasoning for leaving XYZ Corp may be constructive or contentious. Regardless, without fabricating stories, you need to have a clear reason for changing employers. Of those reasons, certain ones may be most effective to share in the hiring process and others not so fruitful or appropriate. Choose wisely and stick with your positive messaging.
- **Walk out in style** - Treat everyone with respect as you inform people of your departure (your superior first), avoiding any discussion of disillusionment or dissatisfaction in your present job. Good for you that you're leaving, but don't rub their noses in it. These are your future references, clients, and an important chapter of your life. Provide adequate notice, so your departure does not leave people in a bad position. Although some employers may immediately show you the door, others will value your smooth transition to your replacement.

When I was 25, I told my boss of six months that I planned to retire when I was 40. He laughed. It was probably really dumb of me, but I put it out there, as an objective I'd set for myself. When I was 36 and reminded my boss it was right around the corner, he laughed louder, as I'd risen to a point of high compensation and honors which people don't walk from. By the time I turned 39, the company had created a part-time position for me during my last year. Then, I walked as scheduled, painfully, leaving something I so enjoyed. But when I left, I knew I'd done it right, having given my all during my time there and not disrupting my company, my teammates, or our clients in my transition. It was the least I could do for the company and the people who had done so much for me.

Once you've gotten your pay rolling, you get to put that money to work. In some cases, you'll have little choice in the matter (payroll taxes) but for most other expenses you'll face a wide range of choices of where your money goes. Our next chapter will walk you through the essentials of spending money, and the tricks and traps which can stretch your dollars and keep you out of consumer hell.

CHAPTER 6

WINNING THE RACE

Winning the Race

> I love money. I love everything about it.
> I bought some pretty good stuff. Got me a $300 pair of socks.
> Got a fur sink. An electric dog polisher.
> A gasoline powered turtleneck sweater.
> And, of course, I bought some dumb stuff, too.
>
> ... *Steve Martin*

For just a few seconds, consider a "toy" you've had your eye on. Something you'd love to have right now, whether you're wearing it, driving it, or playing with it. Call it a guilty pleasure.

As you begin this chapter about spending choices and strategies, you should know that it's healthy to have such interests and the prospect of acquiring something "just for fun". I won't try to talk you out of it, suggest it's wrong, or put some values thing on the topic. The challenge, quite simply, is prioritizing how you want to spend your limited money and having the discipline to avoid purchases that are not your priorities. The choices you can make will put money back in your pocket so you can afford that occasional treat without the guilt trip. There is a cause-and-effect from buying something and there are techniques to allow you to buy more with less.

I often advise wealthy people on this topic and my message is the same as when I advise a family who is struggling with money. The smarter you're about "how" you spend your money, the less stress you will have in other parts of your life. Wealthy people can blow it as much as a poor family can blow it, by living beyond their means and "signing up" for a lifestyle which is unsustainable.

This chapter will focus on the primary expenses of life for a young American, the pressures to buy things and the strategies you can deploy to reduce your cost of living to the level you choose.

True needs - If you've studied psychology, you learned about Maslow's theory of human motivation, or "Maslow's hierarchy of needs". The diagram shows the upward progressions which Maslow believed humans strive for, upon attainment of each lower tier.

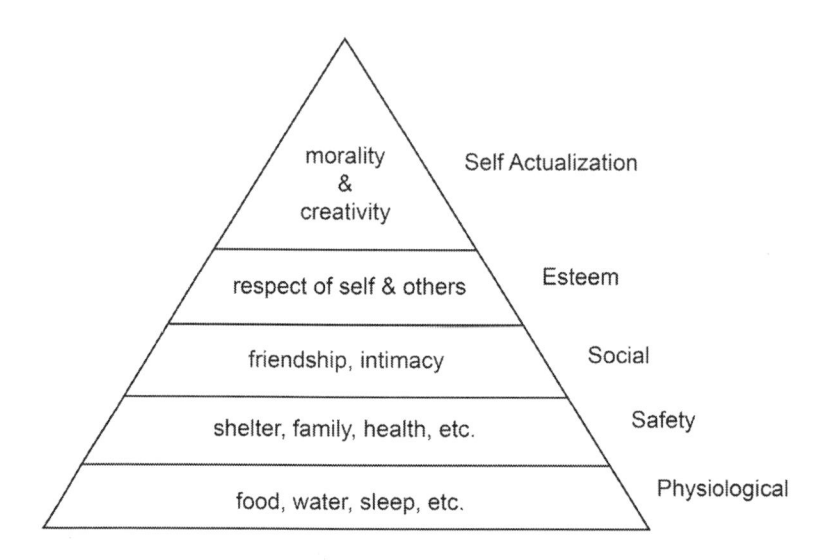

```
                    /\
                   /  \
                  / morality \    Self Actualization
                 /     &      \
                / creativity   \
               /----------------\
              / respect of self  \   Esteem
             /   & others         \
            /----------------------\
           /  friendship, intimacy  \  Social
          /--------------------------\
         /  shelter, family, health,  \ Safety
        /           etc.               \
       /--------------------------------\
      /       food, water, sleep, etc.   \  Physiological
     /_____\
```

Many people's spending decisions are driven like this, with food and water as a first priority, for example, then housing/safety, and so on. Spending challenges occur when the higher drivers are overly pronounced before the foundational needs are truly met. For example, where does a high-end phone, with an expensive data plan fit within this model of priorities? Communications technologies have emerged as a "must have" for young Americans, yet do they deserve precedence over next month's groceries? Do you rationalize the ego of the devise (esteem & social) by convincing yourself that it will help with safety, while forgoing your future financial security because you spent so much on your cell phone you don't have enough to set aside for medical expenses?

The advertisements for products play to all our emotions and "help us" rationalize why we need something NOW. Was that very cool, really thin, really wide, higher def TV really that important, compared to other essentials?

Marketers' covert communications are always lurking, helping you justify your decision beyond the math. You deserve this standard of living, don't you? If you feel that way, you join most other Americans who are caught up in their peers' acceptance, the magnetic draw of products, or the sense that they have fought the good battle and deserve a treat. To get a handle on spending, you have to learn to recognize this dark force and make a pre-emptive strike, using your spending game plan.

Ok, here it comes. You knew that horrible "budget" word was going to be mentioned somewhere in my book. Let's get it out of the way. For many, a budget is a nasty level of accountability and detail mongering which runs counter to the freeform, independent lifestyle young adults relish. You don't want to punch a financial time clock and have to track something all day, every day, right?

Right. Yet, without the budget, you're captive to the draw of all those slick pitches and rationalizing you'll do. Being influenced by others is human nature, as we study others and position ourselves within a broader collective to fit in and strive for acceptance. Yet people buying unneeded stuff at the expense of their essential needs is counter to Maslow's theory. That's how powerful the consumer engine has become since Maslow crafted his theory early last century. Marketers have learned how to twist the consumer psyche to exploit weaknesses, compelling buyers to take actions which are not logical or aligned with their priorities.

That's where the budget comes in, offering a "decision model" on every major purchasing choice. More good news. A budget does not need to be complicated. It's truly simple math, coupled with the discipline to monitor and reference the budget from time-to-time. Remember, you establish it for *You, Inc.* No one tells you how much you can spend. You - and possibly your significant other - determine your spending priorities and what will be done with the remaining funds after your planned expenses are paid.

The next two pages offer a really simple approach to budgeting, using a cash flow tool I developed, used and have shared with others for years.

Monthly Budget

As you'll see below, budgeting is a simple plus/minus exercise. It involves estimating stuff in advance using a "goal", then tracking how you did against that goal when the month is finished using "actual" amounts.

Inflow/Income	Goal	Actual
Salary	$	$
Overtime & Bonus	$	$
Other?	$	$
Total inflow	$	$

Outflow/Expenses	Goal	Actual
Payroll taxes	$	$
Retirement Savings	$	$
Housing	$	$
Food	$	$
Utilities	$	$
Transportation	$	$
Insurance	$	$
Medical/Dental	$	$
Debt Payments	$	$
Cell Phone & Internet	$	$
Clothing & Personals	$	$
Entertainment	$	$
Gifts/Giving	$	$
Other?	$	$
Total outflow	$	$
**Balance	$	$

**Spend, or save for a rainy day?

Use the online budget tool at www.MarvelsOfMoney.org/adults

KEEPING SCORE
TIPS FOR CASH FLOW PLANNING

Big categories work better than tracking minutia. Too much detail will overwhelm the process and you won't follow-through. Account for groceries and restaurants in "food", for example, and everything involved in getting to-and-from places in "Transportation", etc. More detail is unnecessary unless you run into a problem that deserves further detail.

Automate the process using a debit card or mobile payment device which allows you to review an online report of expenses, making it easier to categorize them each month. The cash machine/ATM produces a black hole of unknowns which disallows budgeting. When possible, get receipts for things you buy, using cash to provide a simple record for your end-of-month review.

Review everything a few days after the end of the month, adding up all your expenses for each category each month, reviewing statements and receipts while the transactions are still fresh in your memory. Write the amounts in the "Actual" column and compare with your budgeted goals. Make a business date with yourself, calendar it and keep it. This is an hour or two well spent, as it keeps *You, Inc.* on track.

Adjust things as necessary in next month's budget, tweaking your budget as you learn more about yourself and the world around you. When you're "off" in one category, you've got to challenge yourself to make up for it in another category. If you have an opportunity to make a little more money, maybe you do so. Or, if the income category will be weaker than you'd prefer, it looks like something in the expense area will have to give. Simple math.

Most people who succeed financially use a budget. They don't freak out if they're off a touch each month, but learn and adjust as needed. You're in control and accountable to yourself.

AVOIDING A PERSONAL BUDGET DEFICIT

After you go through the budget process using the cash flow tool, you'll see opportunities for improvement. Most people want more money from income, to spend more on expenses, right? Sure. Yet until you find a way to grow income, you've got to find ways to control expenses so you'll have something left for savings. Here are the most effective techniques to reduce the pressures of spending:

Getting small vs. living large - Yeah, it's cool that you've got 39 features in your mobile phone plan, but are they necessary? You love that morning latte baby, and you deserve it, don't you? Maybe. $3 a day, 7 days of the week, 12 months a year. That's $1,080 you could spend on something you may feel is more important.

When you make more money than you spend on essentials and savings, you enter the realm of discretionary spending. This is when you might get the toy, take the trip which was not in the plan, or buy the very nice gift for someone special. It is where most of us want to be someday, but it's critical to avoid living large, if ever, until your essentials are covered and your future is secure.

> "Too many people spend money they earned...
> to buy things they don't want...
> to impress people that they don't like."
>
> *... Will Rogers*

Stay Ahead on Payroll Taxes - When you're hired, part of the new employee materials you'll review will be your W-4 which you'll fill in for the payroll department to prepare your payroll each period. Some people overstate their "exemptions" on the form, thus reducing their payroll taxes each period, only to owe more money at year end. I encourage you to avoid any sort of finessing of your exemptions, unless advised by a CPA, as you're better off getting a refund than owing taxes at year end.

Pay Yourself First - The reason you see "retirement savings" above other discretionary spending categories in the cash flow worksheet is to demonstrate its strategic importance. A mentor told me to "pay yourself first", meaning do all you can to contribute a portion of each paycheck to a retirement account. My first employer did not have a retirement plan, but a college roommate's brother-in-law pitched me on opening my own IRA (Individual Retirement Account). That was 30 years ago and I stuck $2,000 in that IRA. It has since grown many times that size and combined with my employers' retirement plans it offers a great sense of security to my family. $2,000 was a lot of money that first year I made $25,000 (before taxes), but it felt so good to put the money away where I could not spend it and know I was building a secure financial future.

Let the Buyer Beware - Avoid deals that sound too good to be true. It's really fun to get a great price on something you want, but the "steal" the merchant is offering isn't always what it seems. Often it means the opposite. Deals too good to be true often have one or more of the following characteristics:

- seems too good to be true; a red flag, look closer
- promotes how you'll feel more than the functionality
- offers financing with the product
- offers a free product if you buy another, which usually means neither is particularly worthwhile so they need to tease people into the purchase

Activities & Environment - Build a life around activities which keep you busy with something other than buying and consuming stuff made by others. My girlfriend Lisa and I took up winemaking after graduation. It was a fun and interesting way to spend time together, learn something new, while making something we would enjoy and could give others as gifts. Maybe your thing is biking, helping you to stay healthy and employable, or instead of meeting friends at a restaurant every time you go out, you start a dinner club, rotating to each friend's home each week. Make the event "frugal Friday" and pride yourselves on lean-and-mean dinners, avoiding any sense of opulence. Whatever activities you choose, you'll win as long as they get you off the sofa, out of the stores, and in a zone which supports the *You, Inc.* plan.

Speaking of friends - Friends will go in different directions on lifestyle choices and a ton of pressure can occur if one person is materialistic or financially set and the other is not. Establishing your plan and seeking friends who share your situation helps alleviate the pressures and creates an informal support group to remind you that you're not in this alone. It doesn't mean that you diss everyone who's in a different financial place or in a phase where they're trying to impress, but beware of the side-effects and set your boundaries so you don't get caught up in situations that you can't keep up with.

Speaking straight with your friends about your priorities will reduce the pressure and more often than not, your priorities will be shared by many who've been putting on more of a show than they'd prefer. By leading the way with your honest portrayal, you may help others take down their facade.

Value defined - Companies have latched onto the concept of "personal budget deficit". They mimic higher quality products and services, by dressing up their poor quality stuff with splashy looks, advertising "low cost" to draw in the folks who are trying to save money.

Most American consumers suck this stuff up, falling for the low price pitch. Here's why they end up spending more. Many of the low cost products fail well before their more expensive counterparts, creating a cycle of repeat buying. These companies' product strategies are built upon "planned obsolescence" and the idea that the suckers will keep coming back for the replacement products. That's not innovation but thievery. The negative effects on budgets, not to mention landfills are shocking. You can affect this by avoiding companies whose products and services do not stand the test of time. Save your money for a better product and service, rather than get caught in the consumer cycle which dries up the funds of the poorest in our country.

TCO Analysis (Total Cost of Ownership) - It's easy to get drawn into a product pitch, given a promoted price, not realizing the **total** cost to own something. Let's walk through a few common examples:

- **HOUSING** - Yup, great to own your own house someday, but had you considered property taxes, insurance, and maintenance? Comparing the mortgage payment with your monthly rent provides only part of the answer. Same thing with a vacation timeshare; upfront cost and "low cost financing" sounds great, but what about the homeowner association fees, travel expense to get there, and assessments that will occur when properties require capital improvements?

- **CAR** - Of all American consumer products, this is the purchase that many Americans feel is most necessary and is frequently driven by image. Will you consider the extra insurance cost for that nicer car, or the interest expense on the loan? Is the car best-in-class for reliability, or well regarded for its style? What's the difference, on a monthly basis, between your new car and the cost of mass-transit plus a car share membership?

- **PETS** - Most of us love a pet, most of the time. Beyond the commitment to care for an animal every day and night, have you considered the expenses of food, litter, shots and vet expenses? If you sat in a veterinarian's lobby or talked to one of their staff, you'd be heartbroken at the number of people who learn after the fact that they cannot afford the procedure their pet requires. What do you suppose they do with the pet? Let's see, retirement savings, next month's groceries or pet expense? This is an emotional double whammy, because of your intimacy with your pet. So, I'm not telling you to avoid pets, but go into the purchase with your eyes wide open, and consider the "total cost of ownership".

You'd never know - I learn something interesting every time I meet with an accomplished person. I learn about their background, paths to wealth, and their beliefs which guides their approach to life. Consulting for thousands of multi-millionaires changed my perception about how wealth is accrued and by who.

While reality-TV floods our channels with noise about the flamboyant lifestyles of the rich and famous, the reality is quite the opposite and I encourage you to learn from the truth. Bottom line, most wealthy people do not "show" their wealth in an ostentatious manner. Much of the wealth in America has come from very hard work, great risk taking, and an awareness of how hard life can be without money. Most millionaires live life "below their means", intent on protecting their lifestyle and avoiding financial instability. Generally, they do not want to impress you, nor do they care to advertise their financial success given the predatory environment which preys on fools. This speaks of living humbly, living intelligently, and being just a bit paranoid about the bad guys.

Another fascinating and inspiring wealth characteristic is the background of accomplished people. Many were not raised in perfect homes, did not attend the best schools, and did not take over their parent's businesses. Cool if they did, but the great American dream remains accessible to the disadvantaged, downtrodden, or normal person next door who succeeds through hard work and creativity. With America's millionaire count expected to double to 20.5 million by 2020, the opportunities to participate in wealth building will be substantial.

The long-term health of our nation will be defined by the diversity of wealthy persons and a constructive path for the poor to reach the middle class and beyond.

You've got to spend money to make money - This sounds contrary to my controlled spending tone over the preceding pages, but it's important to grasp the need to invest in yourself. You've gone too far with frugal when you have a crumpled appearance, unreliable transportation, poor physical fitness, or other effects of cost cutting.

Your image, along with your physical and emotional health are the best investments you can make, within a controlled expense framework. Being frugal is great, looking or acting desolate is not.

When To Hire Help - Speaking of spending money, are you the type who likes to have your hands in everything and do things yourself? Maybe it's because you love tinkering on projects, or maybe it's because you don't like to spend money if you don't have to.

Here's my financial logic for deciding whether to source work to others, for example changing my car's oil:

1) Do I enjoy the job? No
2) Can I do the job with reasonable quality? Yes

If I have plenty of discretionary money (excess cash), I'll hire someone to do the work, rather than mess around with something I don't enjoy or I'm not great at. If I'm financially limited right now, I'll continue my analysis:

3) If I were not doing that task, would there be something more effective I could do with my time that would put money in my pocket? If the answer is no, I'll do this job, but if the answer is yes, there is no way I'll do this job. I'll work an hour instead, making up for the small expense with an hour of focused attention to my career.

I encourage you consider these questions above and try to spend your time in the most fruitful way. "Saving money" is not always the answer.

Location matters - Because communities are unique ecosystems, the cost of living can be radically different for two identical lifestyles a few miles apart. Your zip code can affect everything from your time spent commuting (what's your time worth?) to the size of your home given the radically different pricing for housing in two neighboring communities. Insurance rates for homeowner's, renter's and auto insurance protection flux based on local crime and accident statistics. The financial effects can run counter to your desire to live in a nicer neighborhood, or be near your friends and family. These are tough choices that deserve forethought and consideration before signing that lease or accepting that job offer.

I recently discussed the feasibility of moving to Portland with a 24 year old, given their desire to pursue their creative career in Portland. Because of the significantly lower cost of living (housing 40-60% lower in Portland), we determined that given their lifestyle, their new job in Portland could pay $12,500 less per year and financially justify the move. As their job search produced an offer, they accepted a pay level below their former job's pay and came out ahead given the much lower cost of living.

Sometimes the additional expense you're willing to pay to live in one place or another cannot be financially justified but is a way you may choose to use your discretionary funds. If you have no discretionary funds, remember your vision and stick with it. The nicer neighborhood can be in the 5 year plan, rather than the 1 year plan, right?

There's a financial cause and effect to just about everything; understanding the consequences of things allows you to rationalize the worthiness of each choice and stay on-track with your priorities. It's that simple, yet so hard. The influence of mass media and social networking, coupled with the proliferation of cool products and services, puts you at a disadvantage the moment you wake up, listen to the radio, read the paper, surf the web, or walk out the door to have coffee with a friend.

Pace of Gratification - With the speed of media, information delivery and social networks, the proliferation of "convenience stores" and the ability to download your purchase in seconds, it's difficult to ponder your purchases. Vendors have done such a nice job making it easy for us to spend our money! Step back, take a breath, and remember that time is on the side of the negotiator. You're not in a hurry. That outfit, that book (had to say it), that song, or that vacation will neither define you, nor make everyone love you or respect you. It's just a frickin product. Do you really need it right now? Stepping back, you'll talk yourself out of most purchases, or find a better value than the spur-of-the-moment deal.

It is very difficult to "save money" when you are living a good life while indebted to support your lifestyle. Our next chapter will provide an overview of various forms of debt, the reasoning for going into debt, and when to avoid it.

CHAPTER 7

Choose Any Door...

NO DEBT

GOOD DEBT

BAD DEBT

Choose Any Door

I want to start this chapter about debt with the disclosure that when I graduated from college, I had a negative net worth. That means I owed more than I owned. To get through school, I'd taken out student loans for 3 years, with payments due months from graduation. It took me ten years to pay off those loans, but would I do it again? Absolutely. Best investment I've ever made.

Debt can be a powerful strategic tool in wealth creation, as it can magnify the impact of investments, allowing the acquisition of a growing asset while leveraging someone else's money. Yet, for most Americans, the use of debt is non-strategic, accelerating the purchase of something which is not otherwise affordable and drops in value rapidly after the purchase, while the debt lives on. That's the hook many Americans have lunged at, only to be caught for life.

Even after many painful lessons throughout history, it's still easy to borrow money. Fact is, it's hard not to borrow money! The reason? Companies who offer financing make a ton of money on people who desperately want something today that they cannot afford to buy with cash. Whenever an industry can make a ton of money on anything, you'll find a wave of promotion and coercive approaches that tease, tempt and ultimately trap many very smart people. Beyond the "smart people", imagine all the poor souls who have no clue what they're signing up for and how wrong it is to drive them deeper into the ground with financial products they cannot comprehend.

Knowledge and disciplines are needed to avoid catastrophic consumer debt and the magnetic affect of the "buy now, pay later" syndrome. Through greater awareness, you can avoid the lending traps that can cripple your finances, while capitalizing on lending which enables you to build your future wisely.

Why Does Bad Debt Continue to Multiply? - Our country is an incredible blend of humanity from different countries, religions, family backgrounds, and educational levels, all spread across 50 unique states with their own rules and cultural make-ups. What makes this country so damn good also cultivates its greatest challenges and risks. The diversity most of us embrace produces the burden of variation and inability to accommodate everyone while protecting them from who knows what at the same time. Add greed to the inability to regulate every conceivable scam and you get an environment which will regularly reinvent itself to capitalize on consumers.

In 2008, our country's financial systems and capital markets collapsed from decades of unsustainable opulence, financial illiteracy, and failed oversight in government and corporate America. In spite of many government entities and corporations who promote a higher ground, a new cycle begins, earlier mistakes are forgotten, and new dangers emerge. We can blame the government and corporations, but we also have to look in the mirror, as the best deterrent to greed is knowledge. I encourage you to learn how debt works, when it is usually good and when it is usually bad, so you can make informed decisions.

"You're Approved" - When you see this message on any form of email or postal delivery, you can assume it means you have been identified as a sucker for a promotion. No good lender will offer you money without evaluating many aspects of your life, which they can only do with your permission and engagement. I suggest you avoid such promotions, unless you have determined in advance that you want a particular type of credit arrangement for a very specific purpose. Everything else is a waste of your time and puts your personal information in play and your security in jeopardy.

Let's look at types of credit and the logic of why you might borrow for one thing or another.

When and Why? - Many good people and successful companies use debt to achieve their objectives. Again, debt is not all bad. Debt becomes bad when people, companies and governments borrow money to buy stuff which has one or more of the following characteristics:

- High borrowing costs (interest rates and fees)
- Finances a rapidly depreciating asset value (think jeans)
- Cannot likely be paid back with ease

Here's my simplified view on the logic of personal debt.

Credit Rationale Meter

```
rates ↑
                                              Boat
                                              Food
                                           Clothing
                           Car
            College
            Mortgage
        Strategic      Questionable        Weak
```

Thus, certain types of debt tend to carry higher rates of interest, in addition to the weak reasoning for certain types of purchases. There are many points of rationale I have heard over the years regarding people's purchases and related debt obligations. They range from genius to clueless. Fact: if you're financing your clothing, food or discretionary pleasure (think boat, TV, furniture) with consumer loans, you're likely to be in the trouble zone of personal finance.

People who rationalize that their ill advised purchase is a "one time" event, typically have a few more "one time" events financed by the time the first debt is paid off. Such borrowers create a lifestyle which becomes unsustainable without borrowing more money, and that's when they're hooked. Debt and consumerism can be addictive like gambling and drugs, with similar negative effects.

Even if you pay your debt payments on time, you're likely paying high fees for the "privilege" of getting the loan or credit. Such fees are often not apparent. The furniture store which offered "no payment for 90 days" has their cost of capital/money built into the cost of the couch. You get sucked into the "new furniture" syndrome, believing you'll be in great shape in 90 days and "their loss is your win". C'mon.

The smart money is to forego stuff that is not affordable today, unless the purchase is truly strategic and will better position you to earn a living or the asset will rise in value beyond the cost of debt. So, will the outfit really enhance your performance on the job? Sometimes. How about a boat? Most always a pleasure vehicle won't put money in your bank account but drain it for a few hours of pleasure a week. Let's walk through some scenarios to apply this logic to common purchase and debt decisions:

Scenario 1: Chelsea gets a job across town. She could take the bus, but the job calls for varying hours and for customer visits which public transportation would complicate. So, buying a car makes sense to her, as her improved job could allow her to pay off a car loan quickly. All good, as it was questioned and rationalized. Next, the keys for this purchase are to make sure the terms of the loan are reasonable, while avoiding more car than she needs just because of the new job. A car, good. Too much car for the wrong terms, bad.

Scenario 2 - Gerald wants that wider, taller, thinner and more vivid flat screen TV. It will perform better than his present TV, and look very good on the wall of his apartment as guests enter the doorway. His buddies have better TVs, but he does not have the cash to buy one, as he is just getting started in a new job and only a few months into his efforts to become financially stable. He is attracted to a rent-to-own offer from a local electronics retailer, who will charge him a monthly fee for the TV, and apply those rental payments to the purchase prices after 12 months. Sweet!

Actually, not so sweet. When compared to an outright purchase, most rent-to-own "opportunities" are high priced purchases with embedded financing-costs hiding the true value. If Gerald would forego this desire to have a TV *now*, he can save up those monthly payments, paying cash for the TV in a year or two and avoid the hidden financing fees altogether. Those savings can be used for something else which is important for Gerald's future.

Scenario 3: Antonio wants his own house. He's tired of living with other people just one wall away. He's had a good job for the past three years which allowed him to save up money for a down payment. He has no credit problems and can get a low interest mortgage through his bank, producing a monthly payment $200 less than his monthly rent, considering his tax deduction for mortgage interest. However, that $200 savings will be needed for new expenses, such as property taxes and home insurance, so it's a wash (break-even). Add to those costs the maintenance of the home, such as paint and yard care, and the desire to improve the home (new tile, carpet, landscape) and it will actually cost Antonio $100-200/month more to "own a home". If Antonio has a savings account cushion, confidence in the future of his job, and if the home's value is fairly priced given the neighborhood and price history, this might be a good idea. Antonio will give up certain uses of his excess cash for the glory and comfort of owning his own home. Maybe it's worth it. He'll also be accruing equity/ownership in the home, as he pays off the lender over the next 15 - 30 years. If he does not suffer a long disruption in employment during that time.

Decisions like this are not as cut-and-dry as they seem. Risks are always there, yet most peoples' home purchases were made with home loans, rather than all cash. Buying a home using a mortgage loan is often a good idea, if the buyer considers the broader range of variables beyond the emotional play of "I want my own home and real-estate is a good investment". Sometimes.

Scenario 4: Jannae is always tight on cash, even though she's working a full time job. She has payments on her car, rent, plus groceries and other normal expenses. She has the opportunity to go to the beach with her friends for the weekend, but has spent her last paycheck and does not get paid for another 5 days. A couple of financing shops in town offer "payday loans", which will give her an advance payment on her expected earnings in her next paycheck. Definitely not a good idea. Ever. This form of lending is the most predatory, with fees and interest charges worse than most credit cards. The borrowers are not only going into debt, but also using their future pay on top of the exorbitant fees. For someone always short of money, this a never-catch up scenario in the making.

Scenario 5: Hannah is considering a University's on-line Masters program which promotes the degree's career benefit. Maybe. She would need to evaluate the actual benefits of such a degree received from that school. From independent discussions with employers, she will want to learn how much more the employers would pay her, compared with what she earns with her present educational level. With that "potential" pay improvement, how many years will it take to pay off the student loans, plus her time investment, in order to justify the expense? School for the right reasons, great. More school just to add an acronym on your business card and the hope to make more money, probably not so great. For example, as you saw in Chapter 4 "Getting A Job", health care positions are poised for significant growth in the years ahead. They are particularly dependent upon advanced degrees and are expected to offer great stability and pay premiums. Those pay premiums may make the effort and investment in more education worthwhile.

The College Debt Debacle - I'm a big believer in education and the respective investment which is required to build competencies and credentials. Student loans supplemented my summer and part-time school year jobs, allowing me to put myself through school. Student loans have gotten out of whack because:

1. Some schools misrepresent the worth of their degree. The future expense of debt payments surpasses the financial benefits.
2. The loan terms are poor, with variable interest rates, resulting in higher costs and payments than former students can support in their early years out of school. As interest rates rise, so do the payment amounts.
3. Many borrowers quit school mid-stream, for varied reasons, disallowing the benefits which may have been realized by a degree.
4. Some borrowers think they can walk from the future obligation. Not so. The federal government expects colleges loans to be repaid and disallows them from being forgiven, even in bankruptcy filings.
5. The economy has not cooperated, leaving many good people with a burden they cannot support without a decent job.

> PERSPECTIVE:
>
> FEDERAL RESERVE OF NEW YORK
>
> - The outstanding student loan balance now stands at about $870 billion,[1] surpassing the total credit card balance ($693 billion) and the total auto loan balance ($730 billion) in the US
> - $85 billion in student loan debt is "past due" (delinquent) and of that total, three-quarters is owed by people over thirty. More than five million borrowers have past-due student loans.

The Bottom Line: Education is a very personal subject because of its importance in self-worth and the hope for greater capacity to earn an income. Many people experience a diminishing rate of return, as they do not receive the bang-for-the-buck they had anticipated. According to a Pew Research study, the use of student loans for households 35 years and younger has mushroomed from 16% in 1989 to 40% in 2010.

If you are saddled with a student loan, I encourage you to do all you can to structure your cash flow to allow for regular payments, giving up niceties early on. As you are able, work a little extra each year to pay down your loans earlier than required in order to eliminate this drag on the balance of your finances.

> Dear Customer:
>
> Due to your failure to reply, we have forwarded your account onto our collections company.
>
> You're 90 days past due on your payments and due to your failure to communicate......"

Prevention Is Cheaper Than the Cure - We all get in a pinch or mess up from time to time. Some agreements are flexible and interpretive, while others are not. Credit is the latter. When you have agreed to loan terms, whether through a credit card company, car company, a relative, the government, or a bank, the lender expects they will be paid on time. Creditors are not particularly interested in why you cannot pay, yet they would rather have your late payment than nothing at all.

If you're unfortunate enough to have loans which you cannot pay back as scheduled, call ahead of time and candidly describe your situation to the lender. By doing so ahead of time, you're demonstrating responsible behavior in a situation they would otherwise classify as "loan in default", or "increased risk". The lender will likely negotiate terms which allow you to resume payments as soon as it is feasible for you, rather than placing your loan into collections and reporting a loan default to a credit reporting agency. Rather than hoping a debt problem will go away, we can significantly minimize anxiety and pain through candid and timely acknowledgement of the problem.

PRIMER ON LOANS

So, do you still want to borrow money?
The balance of this chapter will provide some essential knowledge and concepts so you can navigate the lending marketplace.

Types of Credit

- **Installment Credit** refers to loans which the borrower agrees to pay back in equal amounts over a specified period of time. Mortgages, consumer finance, and rent-to-own are variations on this theme. Installment loans frequently have set interest rates, which assures specified terms for the duration of the loan. Conversely, borrowers who enter loan agreements based upon a variable interest rate may enjoy an initially lower payment, but risk the rate rising and the higher payments becoming unbearable.

- **Revolving Credit** allows the borrower to borrow up to a specified amount at any time, with repayments occurring at or above a minimum agreed level each month. Credit cards are the most common form of revolving credit. This form of credit allows borrowers to continue to borrow without requiring a new loan agreement: many borrowers maintain high balances on their credit cards and are frequently paying higher interest rates in addition to paying down their debt. Credit lines behave similarly.
- **Pawn Shops and Pay-day loans** are the lowest forms of debt, usually as a last resort for desperate people who have poor credit history or poor financial aptitude. The fees, as a percentage of the money borrowed, are extremely high, for the portion of the population who can least afford them. A nasty cycle.
- **Personal Loans** are worrisome, as they often create personal conflict which overrides the value. Yet, they are used frequently by families to support a loved one. Regardless of trust, if you choose to enter into an arrangement with friends or family, it is strongly recommended that you document loan expectations and treat this as you would any other business transaction.

Start small with credit by opening an account, such as a credit card, which you should pay off in full each month. This will help you to establish your credit history, so lenders are more apt to loan you money when you are ready, such as when you may buy a home. A clean credit history improves your "credit score" which we'll learn more about later, reducing your borrowing costs.

Minimize accounts - rather than opening accounts at various stores, or banks, or on-line providers, reduce your credit accounts to the bare minimum. By doing so, you reduce the administrative burden of tracking multiple accounts and their respective payments, you toughen the rationale for using credit, and you enhance your privacy by not having your data spread throughout the market and with multiple financing companies. If your private data falls into the wrong hands, your credit record can be damaged.

Credit Reporting Bureaus aggregate and dissect data they collect on consumers' borrowing arrangements. These reporting agencies then resell the data to lenders, allowing them to better assess the risk of lending you money, using a credit scoring system. A consumer with a poor credit score may get a loan, but that loan will presumably be priced higher than a low risk consumer's loan, as the lender needs to compensate for higher potential loan losses with their fees.

Consumers who are anxious about their credit ratings have signed up in droves to be notified daily, weekly, or whenever something changes in their credit record. These people are often surprised to learn that when they apply for a loan, the lender does not necessarily use the same rating system or resulting point score. In my estimation, these services are often a waste of money, feeding on people's anxiety over statistics which are inconsistently applied. At a minimum, I encourage you to acquire a free credit report from www.annualcreditreport.com.

> PERSPECTIVE: "IMPOSTER" CREDIT REPORTING WEBSITES
>
> Only one website is authorized to fill orders for the free annual credit report you are entitled to under law — annualcreditreport.com. Other websites that claim to offer "free credit reports," "free credit scores," or "free credit monitoring" are not part of the legally mandated *free annual credit report* program. In some cases, the "free" product comes with strings attached. For example, some sites sign you up for a supposedly "free" service that converts to one you have to pay for after a trial period. If you don't cancel during the trial period, you may be unwittingly agreeing to let the company start charging fees to your credit card. Some "imposter" sites use terms like "free report" in their names; others have URLs that purposely misspell annualcreditreport.com in the hope that you will mistype the name of the official site. Some of these "imposter" sites direct you to other sites that try to sell you something or collect your personal information.
>
> SOURCE: FEDERAL TRADE COMMISSION

Recommended process for borrowing money:

1. **Determine your capacity to borrow** - Rather than depend upon lenders to tell you how credit-worthy you are, why not determine this in advance? Request a free credit report to determine whether you have any problems in your credit history (loans in default, etc) which can affect your rating. Learn the reported score, simply for reference, knowing that lenders will create their own score using multiple sources including the credit report.

   Then, prepare a Personal Financial Statement (PFS). The PFS is a financial snapshot of "You Inc.", providing lenders (and you) with insight to the risk of lending you money. More on financial statements on the following pages.

2. **Identify good lenders** - An important concept from the last chapter was "shopping" for value. Generally, for financial services, I prefer to work with my primary financial provider, a bank, rather than send my personal data to multiple financial institutions just to save a few bucks. Protecting our privacy and the security of our data has become increasingly important given the rise in fraud, embezzlement and identity theft. That said, shopping for fair interest rates and loan fees assures that your institution is offering a fair value.

3. **Submit paperwork/loan application** - Loan paperwork is a bit obtrusive, as borrowers are required to reveal more about themselves and their financial history than most prefer. Yet, as a lender must assess the risk of the loan, such insight is critical to pricing the loan properly and complying with a myriad of regulations. Because of this divulgence of private information, your emphasis on step 2 (above) will allow you to reduce your submission of applications to multiple institutions. The fewer institutions and file cabinets and personnel touching your data, the better.

4. **Establish auto-pay on loan payment** - Rather than mess around writing and mailing a check payment, have the loan payment automatically taken from your bank account on a designated day of each month. This will reduce your risk of a late payment and save you time so you can do something more productive or enjoyable.

A FINANCIAL STATEMENT PRIMER

A PFS (Personal Financial Statement) is an excellent tool for your long-term planning, consolidating your financial data onto a couple sheets of paper to simplify your analysis. Whether you're a huge corporation or an individual (*You, Inc.*), lenders require financial statements.

Here is a description of the two primary components of a PFS:

The **Income Statement** is similar to the budget worksheet I included in Chapter 6, yet consolidates data into higher level categories. A lender does not care how much you spend on food for example. Instead, the lender is looking for "debt coverage", meaning the ability for your income to cover debt payments after other assumed spending needs.

The **Balance Sheet** essentially presents what you "own" and what you "owe". The more you own and the less you owe, the greater your "net worth" and the less risk for the lender, as they presume you are more capable of paying your payments and that you have collateral in event of defaulting on your loan; consider that lenders who are not repaid will seek restitution through seizure of your other assets. Thus, should you lose your job and suffer from depleted income, the lender wants to know that you have additional resources you can tap, or which they may seize. They must pay back their investors and earn a reasonable rate of return on their investment in *You, Inc.* or they will not remain in business.

Updating your PFS quarterly will help you to stay on top of your overall financial condition.

A printable PFS and interactive loan calculators are available at www.MarvelsOfMoney.org/adults

CHAPTER 8 Tradeoffs

Tradeoffs

There's nothing wrong with flipping burgers when you're 70 if that's what floats your boat. But having to flip burgers at 70 to pay the bills is not my idea of a great time.

Most of us have been told at different points in our lives to "save money", but it's such a distant concept given our basic needs **today**. I've been there, struggling to pay rent, afford groceries, buy a piece of clothing, cover transportation costs, while having some fun along the way. Save money for 30-40 years from now? Yeah, right.

Whether you're employed in your "I'll do anything to get started" job, or ramping up with your dream career job, you'll have opportunities to sock away some money. Pennies, quarters, dollars, etc. They add up. You can do it. But you won't do it if you don't have a better reason than people shoving the "you should save money" message down your throat. Truth is, living for today is a trap for people who do not find balance in today/tomorrow. Making a small sacrifice every month allows you to build a strength that reduces dependency, increases your confidence and self-esteem, ultimately leading you to greater financial capacity. Repeated over and over, this rhythm becomes a part of who you are and will enable you to do things **you choose** in the years ahead. That's the essence of financial independence. You may continue to work in your elder years because you want to, not because you have to.

Ok, I'll stop beating the savings drum. What would you say if I told you there is a way for you to put **less** money in savings than others, but end up with **more** than them in the future? I encourage you to study the chart on the next page. It was a game changer for my wife and me and allowed us to retire very young. This chapter will highlight strategies for saving money which will help assure that the only burgers you flip will be in your backyard.

COMPARATIVE EFFECTS
INVESTING EARLIER OR LATER IN LIFE

Year	Early life investor Savings	Early life investor Growth	Early life investor Balance	Late life investor Savings	Late life investor Growth	Late life investor Balance
1	$ 5,000	$ 250	$ 5,250	$ -	$ -	$ -
2	$ 5,000	$ 513	$ 10,763	$ -	$ -	$ -
3	$ 5,000	$ 788	$ 16,551	$ -	$ -	$ -
4	$ 5,000	$ 1,078	$ 22,628	$ -	$ -	$ -
5	$ 5,000	$ 1,381	$ 29,010	$ -	$ -	$ -
6	$ 5,000	$ 1,700	$ 35,710	$ -	$ -	$ -
7	$ 5,000	$ 2,036	$ 42,746	$ -	$ -	$ -
8	$ 5,000	$ 2,387	$ 50,133	$ -	$ -	$ -
9	$ 5,000	$ 2,757	$ 57,889	$ -	$ -	$ -
10	$ 5,000	$ 3,144	$ 66,034	$ -	$ -	$ -
11	$ 5,000	$ 3,552	$ 74,586	$ 5,000	$ 250	$ 5,250
12	$ 5,000	$ 3,979	$ 83,565	$ 5,000	$ 513	$ 10,763
13	$ 5,000	$ 4,428	$ 92,993	$ 5,000	$ 788	$ 16,551
14	$ 5,000	$ 4,900	$ 102,893	$ 5,000	$ 1,078	$ 22,628
15	$ 5,000	$ 5,395	$ 113,287	$ 5,000	$ 1,381	$ 29,010
16		$ 5,664	$ 118,952	$ 5,000	$ 1,700	$ 35,710
17		$ 5,948	$ 124,899	$ 5,000	$ 2,036	$ 42,746
18		$ 6,245	$ 131,144	$ 5,000	$ 2,387	$ 50,133
19		$ 6,557	$ 137,702	$ 5,000	$ 2,757	$ 57,889
20		$ 6,885	$ 144,587	$ 5,000	$ 3,144	$ 66,034
21		$ 7,229	$ 151,816	$ 5,000	$ 3,552	$ 74,586
22		$ 7,591	$ 159,407	$ 5,000	$ 3,979	$ 83,565
23		$ 7,970	$ 167,377	$ 5,000	$ 4,428	$ 92,993
24		$ 8,369	$ 175,746	$ 5,000	$ 4,900	$ 102,893
25		$ 8,787	$ 184,533	$ 5,000	$ 5,395	$ 113,287
26		$ 9,227	$ 193,760	$ 5,000	$ 5,914	$ 124,202
27		$ 9,688	$ 203,448	$ 5,000	$ 6,460	$ 135,662
28		$ 10,172	$ 213,620	$ 5,000	$ 7,033	$ 147,695
29		$ 10,681	$ 224,301	$ 5,000	$ 7,635	$ 160,330
30		$ 11,215	$ 235,516	$ 5,000	$ 8,266	$ 173,596

(assumes a 5% annual growth rate)

> Compound interest is the eighth wonder of the world.
> He who understands it, earns it ... he who doesn't ... pays it.
>
> ... Albert Einstein

Have you explored the power of compounding? In essence, what you saved yesterday earns a little bit of money, making the next day's amount larger, upon which it grows even more than the day before because of its larger base. As that phenomenon occurs over and over, many people end up earning more money in their savings/investments than in their day job.

Take a look again at the simplistic chart on the left page, showing two different savings approaches, each growing at 5% per year. Note that the "early saver" only had to save for 15 years, while the "late saver" had far less money in the end, even after saving for five years longer than the early investor. A version of this chart was posted on an HR bulletin board in my employer's lunchroom early in my career. The exact "amounts" are not the point, but the timing of the savings and the end result are quite important. This showed me the effect of saving early in life, kick-starting the power of compounding while forgoing some initial pleasures.

I liked the idea of "coasting" later in life rather than scrambling as an elder. It helped my wife and me make some tough decisions and hold the line on our budgets, while also setting aside money for having a family. We had a used Volvo that we shared; older and a little clunky looking, but it got the job done. A few friends who chose to buy hot cars straight out of school and take more frequent vacations have shared regrets for not starting their savings earlier. Some feel they'll now need to "work forever".

Over thirty years, we've continued to put money away every year. This approach provided many options as we've aged, including setting aside funds to create and publish this book. Now let's look at how retirement has changed, why you need to "own" the process, and strategies you can use to make saving easier.

It used to be simpler - What happened? The importance of people "controlling" their retirement savings is a recent development in America, as employers or unions historically provided turnkey pension plans to employees. Those plans accrued a retirement benefit for each employee as they met certain tenure requirements. The pensions were generally low growth, company-controlled savings plans that offered a future fixed/flat benefit when an employee reached 65 years of age and retired. Sort of an autopilot program. You just showed up to work and counted on the future pension, plus social security benefits to cover your lifestyle costs upon retirement.

Some companies failed along the way, and corruption in some pensions occurred, wiping out pension benefits for the workers who had toiled their entire adult lives for the company. Although there were some rules and protections in place, regulations only went so far in correcting systemic problems. The world was changing fast.

To pay for their pension plans, employers and unions began to account for future plan expenses in their company's financial statements (of course!). To make up for the monies which had to be reserved for such future retirements, employee's take home pay was reduced, leaving less money in the pocket of the employee on payday. As non-pension, non-union employers began offering higher wages, competition took over (think "free market") and employers began dropping their pension plans in order to compete for the best employees using a higher pay rate. Another phenomenon occurred in the late 90's, as the stock market became more approachable to the average investor and the returns on investment outpaced pension funds' fixed growth rates. Many people wanted to participate in those returns on investment, while increasing their control of the plan, prompting employers to terminate many pension plans.

So, other retirement savings vehicles were born, to allow employees to save money in a more flexible and "self directed" manner. The IRS helped this trend by making such savings tax deferred, thus theoretically reducing employees' tax bill at the end of each year. Such accounts are called 401ks, IRAs (Individual Retirement Account), 403Bs (for non-profit employees), SEPs (for self-employed), etc. They allow employees to contribute a portion of their earnings and invest the money in a manner they choose. Thus, low reliance on the employer, and greater flexibility. Or so it seems.

TIME FOR A REALITY CHECK

The personal savings rate in America dropped approximately 60% since the 1980's, as Americans have failed to transition to self-managed plans. While "flexibility" and "choice" are hot words to young Americans, the burden now falls on individuals to save <u>and</u> manage their investments, rather than counting on others to do so for them. Thus, it's crucial that the right things are being done by the right people at the right time to maximize this opportunity. Following are the primary things you need to know.

Retirement Account Benefits - Money which is deposited into a retirement account can reduce federal and state income taxes each year, thus magnifying the power of compounding. The IRS allows taxpayers to deduct certain retirement account contributions from their taxable income (thus, before taxes are calculated). Then, to enhance this benefit, the assets and their earnings grow tax-deferred for many years ahead, enabling such accounts to grow faster than a comparable taxable investment ("brokerage") account. When we reach the IRS age of retirement and begin drawing from our retirement accounts, we'll be taxed on the withdrawals at that time, presumably at a lower tax rate. This assumes our employment income drops when we enter retirement, thus lowering our tax rate in our presently tiered tax system.

Employer matching - Not that you really needed another reason to save money in a retirement account, but here's a big one: many employers "match" your contributions up to a designated limit. So imagine you save $5,000 this year, and your employer matches $2,000, you just stashed away $7,000, plus tax savings. Sweet!

Automatic Enrollment - The average employee does not have the foresight or discipline to enroll in a savings plan; many lack an awareness of the benefits or are so focused on other life priorities that long term savings are not top of mind. Recent legislation allows employers to auto-enroll employees in plans, which I think is just great. Regardless of what the government dictates, if you join an employer who offers a retirement savings plan, like a 401k, make sure you're signed up immediately and set up a payroll deduction to save as much as you can to get the maximum employer match. If you do not work for an employer who offers such a plan, set up a form of the "Individual Retirement Account" (IRA) on your own, using one of the advisory options I'll outline in the next chapter. Just do it!

Invest appropriately - As you learn in the coming chapter, there are many ways to invest your precious savings. A key miss with many large employer plans is the need for the employee to allocate their savings to the proper investment categories. Often employees fail to take this step, or they ineffectively take a stab at it, given their unfamiliarity with the investment topic. Leading employers are now hiring administrators to provide online tools, workshops and/or educational materials to teach employees elementary investing concepts.

My primary message in this savings chapter is stressing the importance of being invested, rather than just sitting on cash in a bank account which earns less than most other investment choices. In our next chapter I'll recommend a range of investment options for you to consider, including an approach that allows you to place your retirement investments on auto-pilot, so you can confidently focus on other matters.

Seriously question the inclusion of your employer's stock within your savings plan, if you work for an employer who has publically traded stock. Why would you put more eggs in the employer basket, as you already count on them for your paycheck and benefits? Many people have lost substantial money through such inadequate diversification. Sometimes the stock can be purchased below market cost, which can be a great benefit, but then upon the earliest opportunity I encourage you to consider other investments. Don't worry about the perception of loyalty, instead use a range of investments which do not have a dependency upon your employer or industry.

Perceived Wealth Effect on Savings - Global Finance Magazine reports that "households with higher 'perceived wealth' tend to spend more of their disposable income and, therefore, have lower savings rates (a phenomenon known as the "wealth effect"). " Thus, when housing values or the stock market rise, people feel they are wealthy and feel less need to save. This counter-intuitive behavior gets back to the psychology of spending and the planning that helps to keep consumers on track with their spending and savings goals. Have a savings plan and stick with it.

Aging Slowly - Because our medical community is doing such a great job extending lives with improved technologies and practices, we can expect to be around longer than our parents. This creates a need for greater savings than were historically required. The chart I presented earlier in the chapter shows just 30 years of savings. In fact many young Americans who begin saving in their twenties will assumedly work through age 65, which can add 10 more years of saving. That practice will produce a much larger bucket of savings, which will better support a life expectancy of 90 years and beyond.

Retire Early - Really? Not only do you lose the inflow from your income, thus eroding your savings earlier in life, you lose important connectivity to the world when you leave the workforce. Many retirees, like me, go back to work as it represents an important dimension of life. Remember, financial independence means you do not have to work, but may choose to work. More seniors will do so in the years ahead, as they can only play so much golf, or pursue other such interests in retirement, without getting a bit bored. Back to the balance concept: if you have plenty of time to pursue your special interests, you enjoy your career, and you enjoy earning money, why stop?

What about Social Security? - The Social Security Administration reports that among elderly Social Security beneficiaries, 23% of married couples and about 46% of unmarried persons rely on Social Security for 90% or more of their income, with an average monthly benefit of $ 1,262. Take a look at your cash flow worksheet from Chapter 5 and consider how you'll feel if $1,262 a month is all you'll have as an elder. For a person highly dependent on Social Security, it will cover some lower-end housing, a few bags of groceries, a small amount of spending money, along with the medical coverage as allowable by the federal government. How does that dependency feel to you?

Here are a few essential Social Security concepts for your consideration as you develop your savings plan:

- **What is it and how will it help?** - Social Security is a very large federal retirement system, funded from payroll taxes which are deducted from paychecks and from employers' contributions throughout peoples' working lives. As we reach certain designated ages, we become eligible to receive a monthly benefit to help us pay our bills as a retiree. Also, if one spouse passes away or becomes incapacitated, benefits can help families through difficult times.

- **Will it still be here when I need it?** - I don't know, but I expect our country will do what is needed to secure this important "safety net" for needy families. However, because of the small benefit and the concern for the longevity of the program, the last thing you want is dependency on a government program, right? Everything you have read up to this point and what you will continue to read is about **your strength and financial independence;** I look at Social Security as "great if it is there, but I'm not counting on it". That's why I've emphasized savings and retirement accounts, with Social Security being icing on the cake.

Now that we have solidified the importance of saving early in life, how do you invest the money you'll save in order to command solid growth without losing it all? You'll find that investing does not have to be difficult, if you'll spend a bit of time learning a few fundamentals. The next chapter explains the essentials of how to invest your savings, protecting and growing in the best possible ways. You work hard for your money, and it should work hard for you.

CHAPTER 9

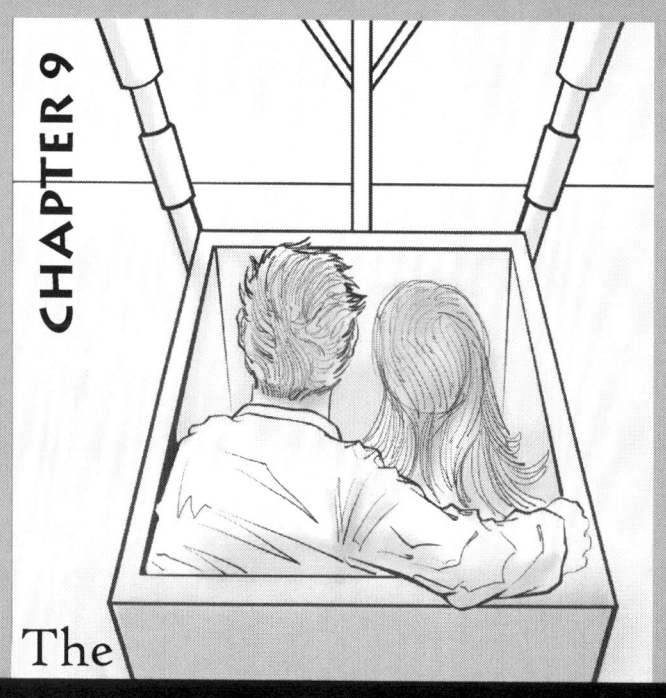

The INVESTMENT CARNIVAL

The Investment Carnival

Once you've accumulated adequate funds in short-term checking and interest-bearing savings accounts, you'll want to invest the balance of your money in longer-term strategies in order to grow the money at a faster rate. Your ability to put your savings to work while you continue to earn money will magnify your financial worth and create many opportunities you may not otherwise have.

Investing is like a carnival; there are many different rides and games for different types of investors. Paralyzing fears or emotional thrills drive most investors' behavior. Although opposites, both result in under-performance of investments. What kind of ride do you like? For most of us, there is a happy middle ground between the roller coaster which promises high growth but potentially catastrophic losses and the Ferris Wheel, which promises safe yet lowly results.

The good news is that you have money to invest and there are many institutions, people and products to "help you". The challenge is that there are so many variations, you can easily make mistakes or become stifled in the process. For too long, investing topics have been unapproachable and intimidating. This chapter will walk through the essentials of investing, offering you insight to the concepts which matter the most, along with the investing strategies even a novice can deploy with great success.

Because this topic can be intimidating, I've structured this chapter in six stages, through which you may advance as you're so inclined. Initially, you can implement fundamental concepts found in the early sections with ease and come back to the more advanced dimensions later.

INVESTING 101 - ELEMENTARY CONCEPTS

Return on Investment - "ROI" is essentially what all investors are striving for, yet one person's definition of acceptable ROI can vary widely from their neighbor's definition. For example, an elder who has accumulated enough money to retire may not want that money put at high risk and will accept a lower ROI than a younger investor who does not mind the risks given they will not need their retirement monies for many years and seek increased growth..

Investment Volatility - Price volatility is a primary indicator of risk, as all sectors ebb and flow with market conditions and news. Volatility generally means the price per share, or what the investor pays to own the investment, swings up and down. Sectors such as small company and international stocks experience higher volatility than many other sectors, yet investors are often attracted to such investments because of their high long term growth.

Diversification - Because various forms of investments behave differently, investors want to structure their portfolios to reduce risk and volatility, while producing an acceptable ROI. When one type of investment is "up", another form of investment is often "down". That may flip-flop the following month, for a multitude of reasons. Thus, many professional investors diversify their investments in order to capture the upside on strong sectors, making up for downside/losses on poor performing sectors. No one gets it right all the time.

Inflation Erosion - Inflation, as measured by the "CPI" (Consumer Price Index) has eroded the buying power of the American dollar approximately 3% per year; if you walk into a store to buy bread this year, you'll get a 3% smaller loaf than you received for your dollar last year. Your investments need to make far more than the 3% lost to inflation, or you're essentially losing money. That's why more volatile yet higher performing investments are recommended for most long-term investors. I'll show you some great examples on a coming page.

INVESTING 102 - DEFINE YOUR PROFILE

Who knows *You, Inc.* better than you? Before you seek assistance with investing, take ownership and define what you can. This will provide a guide for you and the advisors you may hire.

Time Horizon - When will you likely need to withdraw money from the account(s)? For example, saving money for a near-term purchase creates a short term horizon which does not allow for great growth/income of your money. You want such money protected and accessible, rather than at risk and potentially in a down cycle at the time of your near-term purchase. Conversely, if the investments are in a retirement account and you're not going to touch them until much later in life, you can be much more assertive in your strategies for greater growth over the long haul.

Account Type - If your employer offers a retirement account, enroll and contribute as much as your cash flow planning will allow. With a retirement account, however, there is a penalty in most cases when taking out money ahead of retirement age; if you believe you'll need some monies before retirement, you'll also want to open a brokerage account to deposit any excess funds. A brokerage account, managed by you or someone you select, pays taxes on its gains and most forms of income each year. That's ok, but not as attractive as a retirement account (401k, IRA, etc) that does not pay taxes until your retirement years.

Overall Objective - Do you want "steady as she goes" performance, with little volatility and only slight growth? Or, are you willing to see the value of your account(s) going up and down, in order to earn a greater growth over the long haul? For most young Americans, investing for the long haul is best, particularly if a pool of liquid/cash/short term assets is maintained in other accounts (checking & savings).

INVESTING 103 - RISK/REWARD

One of the coolest things about investing is watching investments grow as expected over a long horizon. Following are essential concepts in defining your risk/reward appetite, supported by an extremely insightful chart which Crandall Pierce and Company designed for this book. Their chart shows the annual performance of various "portfolio mixes" of stocks, bonds and cash since 1949, <u>after</u> deducting the rate of inflation (thus "real" returns).

The ride goes up & the ride comes down - There is no sure thing in investing other than the fact that your money is always at risk, regardless of the form of investment. The degree and timing of the risk/volatility is the difference. Scan the 10 different portfolio mixes listed in the right hand column of this chart and you'll see that their average annual rate of return drops as more volatile stocks are decreased and more prudent bonds and cash are increased, going down the page. Yet even the most prudent portfolio mix at the bottom of the page can suffer annual losses during a bad period.

Pigs (in a hurry) get slaughtered - As you can see from the largest loss for each portfolio mix, investors in the most aggressive portfolio lost 9.6% annually for the worst five year period in this history. If an investor is ok with that, and has the time to wait out the anticipated correction, they earn a premium (higher average return) for such risk taking. Yet, many investors jump in and out of the market at a large loss, rather than letting the market's ebb and flow to deliver long term gains.

Balanced Investing Fits Most - Check out the 5th portfolio mix from the bottom, with 40% stocks. Although its average return of 4.2% is much higher than the "prudent investor" portfolio at the bottom, note that its worst return (risk) was better as well. Increased allocation to stocks can produce a healthy risk/reward for many long-term investors who want to make money, balanced with their acceptable level of volatility. Long term investors have historically profited from increased equity use, as reflected higher on the chart.

The Effect of Inflation
ASSET ALLOCATION - RISK & REWARD
Real Five Year Returns
January 1950 - March 2013

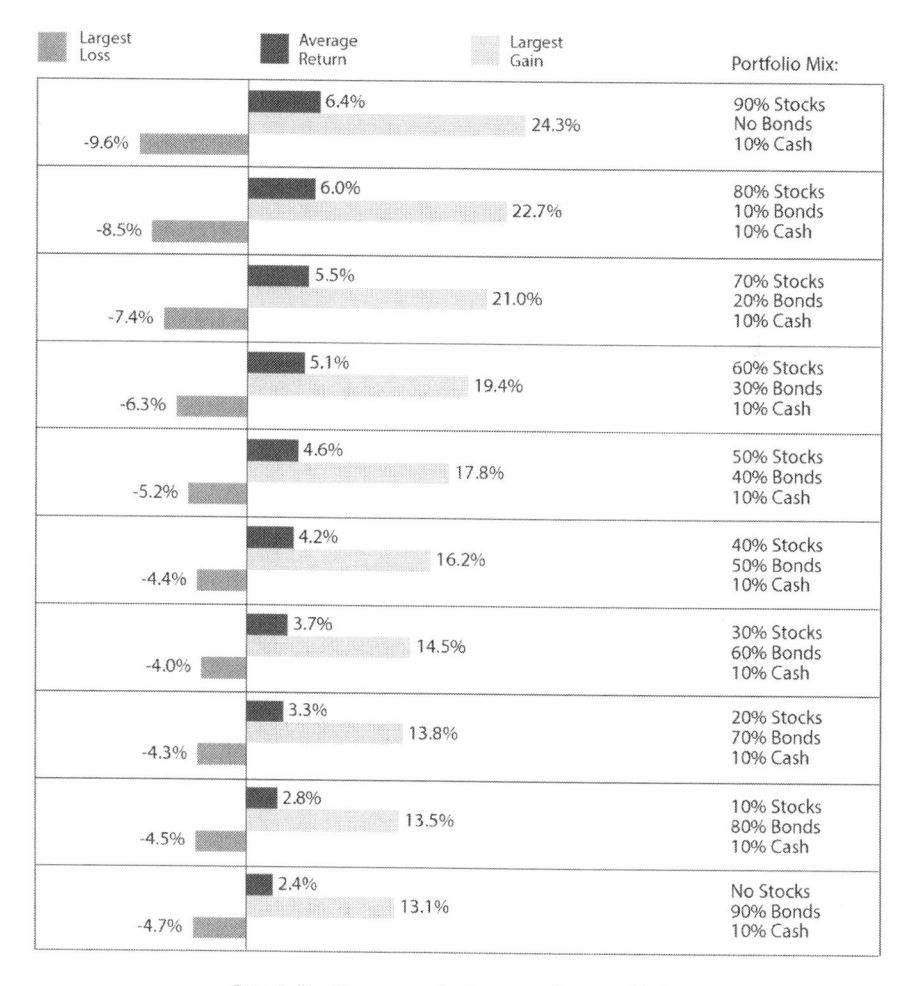

Largest Loss	Average Return	Largest Gain	Portfolio Mix
-9.6%	6.4%	24.3%	90% Stocks / No Bonds / 10% Cash
-8.5%	6.0%	22.7%	80% Stocks / 10% Bonds / 10% Cash
-7.4%	5.5%	21.0%	70% Stocks / 20% Bonds / 10% Cash
-6.3%	5.1%	19.4%	60% Stocks / 30% Bonds / 10% Cash
-5.2%	4.6%	17.8%	50% Stocks / 40% Bonds / 10% Cash
-4.4%	4.2%	16.2%	40% Stocks / 50% Bonds / 10% Cash
-4.0%	3.7%	14.5%	30% Stocks / 60% Bonds / 10% Cash
-4.3%	3.3%	13.8%	20% Stocks / 70% Bonds / 10% Cash
-4.5%	2.8%	13.5%	10% Stocks / 80% Bonds / 10% Cash
-4.7%	2.4%	13.1%	No Stocks / 90% Bonds / 10% Cash

Data: Rolling 5 year annualized returns using monthly data deflated by The Consumer Price Index (69 Observations)

Stocks: Standard & Poor's 500 Stock Index • Bonds: Intermediate Treasury Bonds

Cash: 90-Day Treasury Bills • Inflation: Consumer Price Index

Sources: Standard & Poor's Corporation; Ryan Labs, Inc.; Merrill Lynch, Pierce, Fenner & Smith Inc.; Barclays Capital; Bureau of Labor Statistics; Copyright 2013 Crandall, Pierce & Company • All rights reserved.

The information presented herein was compiled from sources believed to be reliable. It is intended for illustrative purposes only, and is furnished without responsibility for completeness or accuracy. Past performance does not guarantee future results.

INVESTING 104 - MANAGEMENT APPROACHES

Now that we've discussed types of accounts, your unique profile, and different types of portfolios, let's get down to "who" will make the decisions on an ongoing basis. Investors range from active types who make each trading decision, to passive types who engage others to manage investments for them.
As with many concepts in this book,
I'll explain the differences for your consideration.

Self-Managed Investors must make independent decisions, be fascinated with financial and securities markets, and be committed to a consistent and ongoing review of their holdings. If this describes you, then you can open the appropriate account type, define your objectives and begin selecting securities. This is the most active form of investing, and is beyond most people's skills or desire for involvement. Many people who attempt to play the investment game lose because they're not close enough to the industries or financial sectors to move nimbly in and out of investments over time or select the right investment products. Self-managed investors can select just about any instrument for their portfolios, including stocks and bonds. This can be difficult to manage for a young investor, given the other duties of the day and the difficulty managing many different securities with their portfolio.

People who do not relish the day to day duties of investment management should seek help. Let's now consider how to do so.

Mutual funds are "pooled investments" which offer the sale of shares of their fund, like a stock or bond, but which each hold hundreds of securities. The investment decisions are made by a professional management team, and usually around a very specific strategy. For example, I cannot effectively select and monitor companies in emerging foreign markets, so I use a mutual fund to gain exposure in that important sector and am glad to have the help of a professional team focused this complex area.. I'll probably never meet these managers, but I'll buy or sell shares of their fund as my needs change or their performance changes. I like that flexibility. In this approach, I need to select the mutual funds, monitor their performance and ratings, and know enough about investing to do so in a timely way, in order to assure I am diversified appropriately between funds/managers. Investors often have multiple mutual funds, diversifying holdings across many different sectors and each holding hundreds of securities, thus enhancing diversification compared with selecting individual securities, such as shares of stock.

Index funds and **Exchange Traded Funds (ETFs)** are securities you can buy, like shares of mutual fund, but which track every company within a particular sector. When I use index funds to invest my monies, I'm not speculating on the wisdom of the mutual fund manager, because there is no manager! I am instead assuming the return of the broad market ("index") and focusing my management on the percentage of my investment I want in each index. Within different indexes, and ETFs, I'll get representative exposure to many types of companies and countries, yet do so in a more passive manner than the preceding approaches. Many investors mix mutual funds, index funds and ETFs in a single portfolio.

Life Cycle Accounts offer a new approach to helping novice investors stay appropriately invested, without the consummate effort. Name your investment horizon/timeline and the lifecycle account will allocate monies to the appropriate sectors and fund managers. It also rebalances your allocations automatically as you near your "target date" or the markets fluctuate. This is a super passive form of investing, requiring little beyond the initial considerations.

I'm a big believer in life cycle accounts for novice investors who are busy with other parts of life; they often are not effectively allocated because of their lack of knowledge and/or frozen in position because of their discomfort with the markets and the people who are trying to sell them financial products. The life cycle approach can offer the best of all worlds, providing passive management of smaller accounts so you can focus elsewhere in your life. Such accounts also work very well for college savings accounts, as you can name the future year a child will enter college and the allocations will be modified as the child nears college age. As with other types of savings, beginning a college savings account early in a child's life can make a big difference in the future of that child's education.

Investment Brokers typically manage the decisions within investment accounts, so the account owner does not have a day-to-day responsibility. Behind many brokers are brokerage firms which are accountable to shareholders for profits and often driven by incentives to promote products. Brokers can promote investments which may pay them higher compensation than you are aware or which may not necessarily be the best selections for your situation. Because of this, your criteria for selection of a broker to fully manage your investments is critical. As with any industry, there are many excellent brokers along with inexperienced or unscrupulous promoters. You don't want the latter in charge of your precious money.

Financial Advisors have stormed onto the scene to compensate for consumers' desire for holistic financial counsel, beyond investment brokers. Remember, things used to be much simpler, but also much more limited and controlled. Now that your financial and investment options have proliferated, you own more of this responsibility than prior generations did. This, and the public's distaste of the brokerage environment has created a repackaging of traditional brokerage titles and services. Now there are professionals who sell insurance, investments, and provide planning.

You may seek an advisor with financial planning expertise to help you to define and coordinate the many moving parts of your financial life. If so, select an advisor who is truly focused and credentialed in matters other than investments and whose fees you fully understand.

In order to gain access to the services of your advisor, you may be required to use their recommended "high load" mutual funds, or annuities which pay them high commissions and disallow your access to the monies for a designated period of time. If you are not comfortable with their related products, you can avoid this dilemma through a "fee only" certified planner, who advises without any compensation from the sale of products. While it may hurt to pay that upfront fee, getting absolutely independent advice can provide you great clarity. Then, you may select products and advisors for specific investment duties from that well grounded position.

Personally, I don't mind paying others to help me, such as brokers and planners, if I understand the fees and they are justified by incremental improvements in performance or other services I gain as a result. I've occasionally been my own worst enemy, as I would have benefited from the counsel of experts sooner in certain situations. Remember in Chapter 6 I noted that you need to spend money to make money. Same thing holds true on the investment topic, as you do not want to cut corners building your financial security, but you need to be smart about who you are paying and what you are getting for that payment.

INVESTING 105 - INVESTOR TRAPS
Common Investor Pitfalls To Avoid

Avoid Pretense of Expertise - Rather than attempt to beat the investment world, hire help using one of the earlier noted approaches. If you truly have a fascination with investing, set up a small brokerage account to "play" and compare the results against the experts who are managing most of your money. In time, you can always evolve to a self-managed approach if you've truly got game.

Avoid Questionable Stuff - People and investments can be dressed up to look really good for the few minutes you are getting pitched. If the benefits of such a relationship or investment aren't crystal clear and risk/reward well understood, stay away.

Avoid Short Term Mentality - If it were easy to make a bunch of money quickly, don't you suppose everyone would be doing it? A time-proven strategy is to allocate wisely and leave investments alone, rather than jumping in and out of stuff.

Avoid Crowd Investing - As investor extraordinaire Warren Buffet has said, "Be fearful when others are greedy. Be greedy when others are fearful." By the time people are talking about a hot idea, the big money is generally in the hands of the early investors and new money is generally at greater risk from the higher price of the investment as the crowd jumps on the bandwagon.

Avoid Sporadic Investing - Constantly add to your investments, both retirement and brokerage, in order to build your portfolios over long periods of time. This approach buys into each investment at multiple price points, rather than going "all in" on a single day, which is often driven by greed.

__INVESTING 106 - DEEPER ALLOCATIONS__

Let's now build upon the earlier diversification concept, when you learned how a few example asset classes can be combined and how they perform differently over time. Many other asset classes could be added to the chart, to provide even **greater diversification.** As you are interested in a deeper understanding of diversification, following are additional types of asset classifications to invest in, providing exposure to many parts of the market which produce varying types of returns and volatility. Also, within each asset class, there are subcategories which behave uniquely. Blended, such configurations produce varying levels of growth over time, with less volatility than a fewer number of asset classes.

Stocks, Bonds, Real-Estate, Cash - Broadly, traditional investments are comprised of these four categories. **Stocks/equities** are slices of the company sold to investors. Investors expect to make money from the growth of the stock price coupled with dividends paid out along the way. **Bonds** are issued by companies and governments with a commitment to pay a certain rate of interest to the investor, then pay back the investment in its entirety at the end of a period of time. A **REIT** (Real Estate Investment Trust) invests in many properties and behaves like a stock, selling portions of itself to investors, while also paying regular dividends. It's a way for an average investor to own real estate, without the consummate headaches of managing property or over-committing to a single property. Investment **"cash"** refers to monies not yet invested, but earning interest, commonly in a money market fund.

Precious Metals & Commodities - A more obscure, albeit sexy asset class, precious metals and commodities are examples of assets you can invest in using the strategies outlined earlier. Some securities are more dependent upon investor sentiment than the supply-and-demand characteristics of commodities. For example, gold pricing is driven by doomsayers and broad concern for world currencies, with gold being the presumed fallback/safeguard, yet it has little industrial value. Conversely, commodities have broad use in day to day life, as their prices naturally rise and fall as global demand changes.

For precious metals and commodities, avoid direct ownership of one metal or one commodity, but rather use a fund or ETF to provide broad exposure to many components of that asset sector. Remember, everyday experts are mining these sectors looking for pennies of value and positioning for swings months ahead of average investors seeing such trends in the news. To attempt to compete with such focus requires as much focus and a lot of luck.

Growth, Income, and Value - Within each asset class, companies and securities are generally structured to perform in 3 ways. Some companies are structured to *grow* which requires them to retain their earnings, reinvesting the earnings in new products, markets and sometimes in the acquisition of another company. They do not tend to distribute their earnings as dividends to investors. Because of their anticipated growth, they're often expected to rise more in share price than companies who distribute their earnings along the way.

Income investments are distributing their earnings more regularly and thus not as focused on growth. Investors who want or need income along the way select income investments, which usually means dividend paying stocks or bonds paying interest.

Value investments offer upside/growth in the value of the security, as the market increasingly appreciates the virtues of a company or entire industry which was/is going through a difficult phase. This could be a single company's product recall, for example. Great company, great products, yet investors run for the hills when an alert is issued on a bad product and they sense risk in the future. Value investors seek companies or entire sectors who have suffered such reaction, yet have characteristics that bode well for the future.

Hedging - Hedged investments essentially bet against the common market sentiment. For example, a hedged investment may speculate that a particular industry will go through hard times in the years ahead. A hedge can be developed for just about any contrarian view, as people are willing to bet against the market. Investors are increasingly using hedging instruments to reduce the downside risk in their portfolios, following the catastrophic losses suffered in 2008/2009.

Size of Company - Investments behave differently based upon the size of each company. Size is driven by sales and profitability, but the key metric is "market cap" (capitalization), meaning the value of the company's shares of stock held by investors multiplied by the present share price. As an economy goes into recession for example, larger public companies have resources, management depth, and product power to weather a storm better than many smaller companies. In difficult environments, investors often flock to such high quality larger companies who are apt to perform better than their smaller counterparts. In other market cycles, smaller companies outperform larger ones.

Industry - Rather than invest in ten different companies in a single industry, such as telecommunications, I want exposure to technology, energy, healthcare, business services, etc. Certain industries fall out of favor, while others become the hot sectors. Because we cannot predict cycles as well as we'd like, it's good to have many industries reflected within our investments. In 1998, I over-invested in technology stocks and when the internet crashed, my losses were magnified because of my concentration to one sector.

Location - The U.S. has a solid economy, compared to most other parts of the world. That said, many parts of the world are growing faster than the U.S. and there are foreign companies which are expected to exceed the performance of American companies. I want some of that! In my retirement accounts, for example, over 30% of my investments are in foreign securities. Of the many American companies I invest in, most have significant foreign sales, thus adding to my portfolios' global diversification.

Private Investments - Small businesses in America are funded primarily from their founder's assets, cash flow from operations and friends and family. That's where you might come into the picture. Might you choose to invest in a friend or family member's business or innovative idea? If so, note that such an investment is rarely regulated and monitored, other than what you are told and accept on trust.

More often than not, such investments do not return investors' capital, much less the rate of return that is commensurate with such risk. Until you are a very seasoned investor, consider such investments as charitable acts, rather than prudent investing. Another way to participate in such investments is with your services. Possibly through your expertise, you are able to offer "sweat equity" rather than capital to the business to help them reach the next level. Even then, such investments are highly speculative and becomes the source of many soured friendships when businesses fail.

Another form of private investment is investment real-estate, or a partnership interest in real estate. As with other investments, purchasing a property may work, but you should consider that as a younger investor without much capital, you would find the investment constitutes a disproportionate share of your estate. When you add such real-estate to the personal residence you may own or hope to own, the real-estate asset class would surely be over-weighted in your financial picture, putting you at risk. You also may incur the burden of management of the property, which requires time and expertise. I feel real-estate is an excellent investment, but for the vast majority of young Americans, a passive approach using REITs is a better way to go, until expertise and other financial developments mature within your estate.

In closing, how can you possibly figure all this out and make really intelligent choices? Maybe you can't. Ok, you probably can't. There, I said it. Most people fumble through these murky matters and need help. I encourage you to either establish a lifecycle fund or hire a professional aligned with your objectives to help you in your journey.

Speaking of getting help, most people evolve through various forms of relationships as they establish financial independence. Relationships can have good and bad financial consequences, so our next chapter will walk through approaches to reduce financial stress from relationships.

CHAPTER 10

IT'S COMPLICATED

Client Intake Form

Thank you both for coming to my counseling office to discuss your interest in building a relationship with each other. In advance of our session, I ask that you complete this questionnaire:

Are you two friends, significant others, or married?

What is the income difference between you?

How many other adults reside in your household?

How many of those adults are your children?

How many of those adults are your parents or siblings?

Do you share or separate expenses with cohabitants of your home?

How many persons in your home are dependent upon you?

Have you decided to share or separate financial affairs?

What are the divisions of duties in your household?

Are you aligned on family, social, cultural, political, physical, intellectual, career and financial dimensions?

Do you seek a long-term relationship which will weather all storms, or are you ok with making a commitment and then backing out if your feelings change?

You may not have clear answers to all of these questions, but we will discuss each item in our sessions together.

It's Complicated

It's great to be self-sufficient, getting to a point of supporting numero uno and looking at no one other than yourself in the financial mirror each month. For many, it's a life they choose, yet challenges arise when an illness or injury erodes earnings, or duties require more than one person's attention, or a lack of shared expenses produces a higher cost of living. As one in three baby boomers are single and experiencing these very difficult scenarios as they age, many younger Americans will be motivated to create a better life as they watch the challenges unfold.

In fact, our world revolves around people with interdependencies, by predicament and by choice. In a perfect blend of consistent compatibility and coordination, the pooled resources of a couple can create a secure and efficient homestead for a lifetime of comfort. Yet as we know, there is rarely a perfect blend, when consistency, compatibility and coordination are required from two or more human beings in a rapidly evolving world. Regardless of good intentions, personal and situational changes constantly stress the plans and dreams of all people, compounding the complexity of financial planning.

This chapter will review multiple forms of relationships and the dynamics that commonly affect finances. By considering the implications and effects of relationships in advance, you can reduce some of the angst which will naturally occur. Even then, you're counting on good fortune to blend with your reasoning skills to improve the odds that your relationship will work out, or at worst have a neutral effect on your finances. Millions wish they were so lucky, but it's complicated.

Moving beyond you usually begins with a roommate, in order to share resources and enjoy each other's company. This arrangement provides each person with a great education about likes and dislikes, roles and responsibilities and the daily effect of "someone" being in your space, without having to commit to them for life. In spite of that detachment, roommate dilemmas can be just as traumatic as marital discord, and household move-ins and move-outs can be expensive.

I'll assume you will select a roommate based on a sense that you will be comfortable with them. But in order to avoid costly disruption from a failed living arrangement, you've got to go beyond that feeling and ask some tough questions of each other. Here are some expectations to establish in advance of receiving your first cable bill:

1. Agreed split for all bills. What is shared and what is not?
2. Household schedule. How late are TV, music, or video games going? Are work schedules compatible?
3. Who does the shopping, cooking, and cleaning? Are you going to be separated on all fronts other than the shared roof, or will you split duties based upon skills or preferences?
4. Parties and overnight guests. Yeah, how much do you want other people in your home who are not paying rent?
5. Alcohol, smoking, drugs. What are your values and boundaries?
6. Privacy is defined differently by people. What aspects of your life, including your bedroom, computer files, phone, etc, do you consider highly private?

You can walk from many mistakes in life, but there's a weird feeling that takes over when you've got conflict in a household. Also, by agreeing to the ground rules, you're able to budget without surprises and avoid the interpersonal conflict that arises when business agreements are not defined in advance. If your roommate is your significant other, you'll have many other matters to deal with, which makes these initial expectations even more important. By getting these elementary items settled, you're in a better place to then handle the relationship stuff that occurs in more intimate relationships.

Marriage builds on experiences from friendships, roommates and significant others, adding complexities. Approximately 50% of first marriages, 60% of second marriages and 70% of third marriages in our country end in divorce, producing residual damages for young Americans. Before locking in a commitment for life, many young Americans are striving to do so from a more experienced and knowledgeable position than prior generations.

The National Survey On Family Growth's 2010 study reports cohabitation up markedly since its 1982 study, with marriages starting later in life (25.8 for women and 28.3 for men). To increase the probability of a long and happy marriage, consider these added financial dimensions to determine long-term compatibility:

- **A Shared life vision** goes well beyond likes and dislikes. Would it be so bad for each of you to go through the life vision exercise in Chapter One and compare notes? Maybe you've done a flavor of that through conversations over dinner and don't need a piece of paper, but it's important to understand the hopes and dreams of your lifelong partner to assure you are reasonably aligned. Marriages are commonly torn apart by misalignment of priorities and values. Such differences can have marked impact on finances and the resulting personal conflict.
- **Financial capacity** can be different for each person, but it is important to define up front whether or not you will comingle your estate and affairs. I assume most will combine all affairs, as young Americans don't have much to separate and it's a thrill to build something together. However, if there is a significant difference in wealth and earning capacity, some couples establish pre-nuptial agreements to separate and protect one person's wealth until such time as greater trust is established. I feel fortunate to have been poor at the time of my marriage so the topic was a non-issue.
- **Financial competencies** should determine who does what in the management of financial affairs. Rather than assuming anything, get to know each other's skills, so roles and responsibilities can be defined and mistakes or disagreements can be minimized.

- **Financial history** microscopes the baggage each person may be dragging into the relationship. Not saying it's a deal-breaker, but as with everything we are discussing, shouldn't you know how a future spouse has managed their financial affairs in the past? If they have a credit problem, which you may inherit through your relationship with your new "cosigner", do you want to first learn about it when you're turned down for your first mortgage or attempt to enter into a rental agreement? Such negative surprises don't work out so well.

> "Everyone wants to ride with you in the limo,
> but what you want is someone who will take the bus with you
> when the limo breaks down."
>
> ... *Oprah Winfrey*

When stuff goes wrong financially for one or both spouses, it can flow over into other areas. The stress from reduced pay, lost jobs, financial mistakes, mounting bills and investment losses can push even the best relationships over the edge. There are a few ways to reduce the damage from such unfortunate events.

Communication is first and foremost. Too many people hide their struggles hoping they'll go away, because they're ashamed of failure or concerned for the negative effect on the relationship. Confront bad news quickly and in a thoughtful, clear way. The best marriages will work through challenges together and determine what can be done to avoid such a problem in the future.

Break it down. Discuss factually where things are, how they got there, and what you are concerned with. This will provide an outline for the steps that can be taken to fix the problem and move forward. This also provides the guide to avoid the problem in the future.

<u>Move on</u> and avoid rubbing the other's nose in the dilemma. Great marriages shouldn't be guilt factories, but support structures for two people to work through life's odd situations together. If the problem reoccurs and a spouse continues to put the household at risk, professional help is required and I encourage you to engage that help early in the marriage rather than allow an impasse to develop.

A scheduled monthly financial meeting can eliminate problems that otherwise well up and become bigger than they need to be. You don't want your relationship to be driven by finance, yet it's a crucial component and should be a proactive rather than reactive process. In such a meeting you can hold each other accountable for reconciling accounts, review the monthly cash flow, discuss financial topics and needs on the horizon, etc. From that, agree and write down who will do what over the coming month outside of traditional duties, then start next month's meeting with a review of the status/results from that list.

Now, these approaches to managing financial concerns can be applied to other challenges in a marriage, and in life for that matter. My wife and I have failed on numerous occasions, while struggling with life's bad breaks along the way. It's amazing how mutual respect, coupled with straight-forward and candid communication solves most challenges.

So, you want to have kids? We have three kids and I can't imagine life without them. They're 18, 23, and 25 years old as of this writing and we've learned as much from them as they've learned from us. But no one taught us about the finances of a family and the cost of raising a child. I recall my surprise many times while discussing our family's escalating expenses with my wife, who manages our budget.

Families spend more or less on their children given their income bracket. The USDA reports "A family earning less than $59,410 per year can expect to spend a total of $169,080 (in 2011 dollars) on a child from birth through high school.

Similarly, middle income parents with an income between $59,410 and $102,870 can expect to spend $234,900; and a family earning more than $102,870 can expect to spend $389,670." This does not include college, which can cost well above $100,000 for an in-state four year college, and double that for a private college.

Having kids is awesome, when you're ready. Even then, it's a big job, with personal priorities requiring change and a great deal of emphasis placed on the kid(s). Financial stress can be compounded quickly with the additional care and expenses, so my encouragement is to plan for such time and expenses, prune parts of your life which are not as important to you and work hard together to maintain a family for life.

Although my wife manages our household full time, being parents has still proven challenging at times, so I have a great respect for single parents. My consulting experiences have shown me the effects of divorce on families' finances and it is never pretty. When two adults' earning capacity is split in two and their cost-of-living is magnified because of the duplication of expenses, the capacity to support the family's daily interests and still have money to save for retirement is jeopardized. These negative consequences are dwarfed by the personal struggles resulting from family fragmentation. One of the greatest opportunities in America is the resurgence of the family and the long-term commitment of couples to stay together to raise their children and beyond.

Parents, family and in-laws have an interest in your marriage, naturally. They can provide guidance and support, or totally undermine your relationship. Much as couples need to establish ground rules for themselves, they need an understanding about what works and what doesn't as it relates to family members. The most common points of conflict include frequency of visits, the desirability of drop-ins, invoking opinions, and the privacy of your affairs.

Family business arrangements magnify the financial complexity of one-on-one relationships. The decision to help a family member financially, or to enter into a business agreement with a family member, is quite personal and varies widely by background, culture and circumstance. Regardless of your beliefs, my strong encouragement is to support your family philosophically, emotionally, and through shared resources to the degree it does not put your immediate family at risk. Then, should you choose to provide financial support, do so with a clear understanding of outcomes, time-frame, and the dollar limit you will set for such support.

Compassion for others is a personal choice and I'm not suggesting you become Ebenezer Scrooge. In fact, if you look back at the cash flow budget worksheet in Chapter 6, you'll see a monthly spending category for "Gifts/Giving". Of course sharing is important, but you've got to have a boundary on such gifting/giving or you'll put everything else at risk. Your discipline on this topic will allow you to affect more people with your resources more effectively over time. This is a good discussion to have with yourself and with your partner/spouse before the need arises.

Speaking of giving and compassion, our next chapter discusses the needs throughout our society and the many ways you can help. As with a call for help from a family member, the calls for help from community and social causes are difficult to deny. Planning your approach to helping will improve your quality of life and your impact on society as well.

CHAPTER 11
BEYOND YOU

Beyond You

As I walk down the sidewalk and see a panhandler ahead, I subconsciously scan for an alternate path and then consider my response if I'm confronted. I don't carry change.

Driving up to the intersection, I see the couple who stakes out each side of the exit ramp with their "anything will help us get home" signs. As I've done for the past year with this couple, I quickly reach for my phone to appear busy as she walks by my window to the outstretched hand at the next car.

Reading a popular magazine while waiting for my doctor appointment, I flip rapidly past the page with the picture of the beautiful child with the cleft palate. Having seen the plea for help in the child's eyes before, the image is now permanent.

As I scan the 47th charitable mailing received thus far this year from someone I do not know, I briefly consider opening it. It clearly contains an invitation to a social event, golf tournament, or auction to raise funds for an important community cause. I place it unopened in the "charitable requests" folder for later consideration.

My callous approach for dealing with random charitable requests protects me from the deep guilt I feel when not helping every person and answering every need which calls out. I'm overwhelmed and occasionally disturbed by the profound needs in our world and the sense that I am too comfortable when others are not. Requests for community support come regularly from family, friends, friends of friends, schools, churches, people I just met last weekend, along with the five social services organizations which currently have my attention. I can't save the world, but I truly wish I could.

"The test of our progress is not whether we add more
to the abundance of those who have much;
it is whether we provide enough
for those who have too little"

...Franklin D. Roosevelt

Accept It. From childhood, my parents began my life guilt journey by reminding me whenever I turned up my nose at food that "people are starving in China". As I grew up, that feeling magnified as I learned people were also starving just down the road. When we consider the poorest in our most fortunate country, their healthcare, dietary, housing, and other essential service needs are beyond comprehension. Poverty is not a modern phenomenon, yet in our age of information and the speed of media, it's quite vivid. To counter the stark reality, I leverage my capabilities and resources to make a difference in a structured, albeit mechanical way. Here are things to consider as you determine how you may choose to make a difference.

Get Passionate about something! Of all the world's problems, which one would you most like to solve? Or, closer to home, might there be a program which was particularly important in your formative years or when you struggled at some point in the past? Pick a cause which really pulls at you, rather than meekly signing up for something just because a friend suggested you get involved. Unless you're really interested, you'll have a hard time committing and can feel bitter when you are grinding on a community task at the expense of something else.

Consider your assets before you make a gift. Do you have plenty of money, or plenty of time? Most young Americans have more time than money, so why not provide services rather than cash? Non-profits are desperate for volunteer help in order to keep their payroll costs down and engage new community members in their mission. Thus, a perfect fit, as long as expectations are clear regarding your contribution going in.

Beyond having excess time to give, your relevant assets include many of the skills and personal traits you laid out in your resume and would present in a job interview, per Chapter 5. As with a job, you are attempting to find a good fit for your talents and the non-profit's needs. This is a straight-forward discussion you can have with a member of their leadership team, a Board member and/or another volunteer. Consider starting out by attending one or more of their functions or viewing a program being delivered in order to see the organization in action. From there, you can determine how you want to be involved and the level of commitment you can make.

> "There is no exercise better for the heart
> than reaching down and lifting people up."
>
> ... John Holmes

NPR (National Public Radio) compiled hundreds of service examples in their program "Participation Nation", highlighting a wide variety of caring services and creative approaches people are taking throughout America to help one another. The diversity of the needs and the grass roots efforts of the participants epitomized the power to help without requiring big organizations to do it all. For others, plugging into a larger, well structured non-profit provides a turnkey approach to helping. For example, my friend Marcus delivers "Meals on Wheels" to people in need throughout our city, driving a 90 minute route to deliver 8-12 meals which he picked up from the non-profit's central kitchen. It's a compassionate outreach, without judgment or expectations of the recipient. Another friend, Gary, works for one week each year building a home for a family in need, as part of the Habitat for Humanity mission. He tells me it is an incredible feeling to build the home with teammates and within a week hand the keys to the future homeowner, who participated in the construction and will finish the interior with other volunteers. Wow!

Due diligence will enhance the impact of your charitable time and money. Should you choose to become affiliated or offer financial support to a community cause, it's wise to evaluate their track-record and standing in your state before committing. Under guidelines issued by the Better Business Bureau (BBB), charitable organizations "should dedicate at least 65% of their funds to charitable programs, with no more than 35% toward administrative and fundraising costs".

To point, the State of Oregon's Attorney General publishes its annual "20 Worst Charities" listing to teach donors what happens to their financial gifts when charities are not well researched. 2012's list includes charities with "Breast Cancer Foundation", "Firefighters Support Foundation", "Committee for Missing Children" and other emotion-filled missions embedded in the name of the charity. Yet, these "20 Worst..." only spent 2.7% to 21.7% of the funds they received on the supposed recipients of the charity, rather than the 65% BBB minimum, with the rest going primarily to compensation of their staff and fundraising expenses. There are enough community organizations delivering great results year after year that there is no need to share your resources with those who would squander them.

To determine the credibility of a charity, you can research them through the Better Business Bureau's web-site at www.bbb.org/us/Charity-Reviews, where you can enter the name of the charity and location to determine whether they are "BBB Accredited". If not "accredited", your red flag goes up and you would want to establish a logical and compelling reason to give to such a charity. An example might be a special fundraising drive for a local cause, which may never be BBB Accredited because the initiative is short term or quite small, yet you feel it may be worthy of a gift.

Today's largest donors have hit home runs with their professional careers and business successes. They have been raised in an environment steeped in performance expectations and do not see their charitable interests any differently. If they are to associate their name and their hard earned money with a cause, they want to understand the impact of their dollars and see the results in action.

The significant creation and distribution of wealth referenced in Chapter three will produce a force in giving that the world has not seen, spawning many capable donors. Well run charitable organizations will capture many of those gifts and improve the lives of millions of people throughout the world. The collective effects of many small gifts will also be important.

> ### Perspective: Millennial Engagement
>
> The Millennial Impact Project reports that about 75% of 20-35 year old people participating in their study said they gave money to a nonprofit in 2011, while 70% said they have helped solicit donations by encouraging colleagues and others to support a cause. Of young adults who gave money to charities in 2011, 58% reported that their largest contribution was $100 or less. 90% said they volunteered for a non-profit during the year.

How much is enough? Many religions stipulate gifting levels based upon income, or alternately discourage the accumulation of wealth. I've consulted with people who espouse that "charity starts at home!" and thus have no intent of gifting outside of their families, while others gift all excess funds to charities. How much you give is a highly personal choice based upon a broad range of variables. My philosophy is to first build financial capacity to enable greater long term giving, as long as such rationale does not become a lifelong excuse for hoarding our money. Again, it is a delicate decision which is deeply personal so I'll leave it at that.

Budgeting your gifting will help you avoid making commitments you will regret upon reflection. Remember, just about every request is a tear jerker or a compelling cause you can support. That's the challenge, so setting the budget in advance negates over-gifting, just as such a process provides a guide for your lifestyle spending. Your firm budget (dollars and/or time) also allows you to say "no thank you" with confidence when fundraisers are knocking on your door and you want to avoid the guilt trip. You have a plan and are sticking to it.

For many, a payroll deduction is a great way to simplify financial gifting through an automated routine. United Way, for example, continues to market its very broad community initiatives to employers, who often set-up workplace programs to encourage employees to participate in supporting their programs. Alternately, you can make a direct gifts throughout the year, as important community needs arise and you may seek a closer connection with the charity, rather than donate through a group program. Charitable gifts are often tax deductible, which increases the capacity to give through tax savings. This process does not have to be rocket-science. Follow your heart, balanced with reason.

> If you want 1 year of prosperity, grow grain.
> If you want 10 years of prosperity, grow trees.
> If you want 100 years of prosperity, grow people.
>
> ... *Chinese Proverb*

Mentoring is emerging as a very impactful approach to charity, as people in need can only learn so much from a stipend or a group program. Many social problems are associated with a lack of connectedness to mentors, as a result of broken families and limited social services. If you look at teenage crime, a 25% high school dropout rate and the plethora of other maladies affecting American youth, you will find a pattern of pain and distrust. Throughout the country, millions of kids would benefit from a weekly adult visit and could develop a sense of trust and hope from that limited experience. Left to their broken environment, they may get to a better place, but it is more likely if a kid has a friendly connection with someone like you. Can you imagine the trickle-down effects of helping a kid become a productive and positive adult?

> The simplest acts of kindness are by far more powerful than a thousand heads bowing in prayer.
>
> ... Mahatma Gandhi

You get a lot by giving. Whenever I spend time helping someone who's struggling, I walk away inspired. I feel good and I want to do more. It doesn't feel obligatory. Giving money to others is important, as we are able, yet when we serve others, we gain in the process. Outcomes include developing a greater appreciation for our own good fortune, while increasing our empathy for others. The humility we gain through personal interactions flows over to other parts of our lives, improving our outlook.

When serving others, you also benefit through your development of new skills, which can be powerful assets to *You, Inc.* in your career and personal life. The Bottom Line is that our country's support for people in need must go far beyond government programs and the de-motivating effects experienced by many people when they receive government entitlements yet lack personal connections and guidance. Individuals like you can magnify taxpayer impact by providing relevant, caring interactions with people who need it the most.

Many people reach a point of need because of bad circumstances and mistakes they've made. Each of us is just a step or two away from similar personal calamity. Our next chapter describes the most common risks in our financial journey and how you can avoid taking the wrong turns ahead.

CHAPTER 12
"JEOPARDY"

Jeopardy

You only have to do a very few things right in your life, so long as you don't do too many things wrong.

...Warren Buffet

Financial pain often comes from seemingly unrelated issues. Imagine that you've done just about everything right financially, yet the fruits of your labor are taken away because of one bad choice you make, a personal challenge you had not addressed, or an act you could not control.

Our country's courthouses, hospitals, rehab centers, and counselors' offices are full of people in need. Some are attending to their affairs from a position of strength, yet most enter in a state of weakness, having messed up or been hurt by someone else. Once promising lives can get caught in a nasty web, deferring financial independence. I'm referring to young Americans out of school and on their way to a very good life. Educated, employed, possibly married, but derailed for some reason. Most did not see it coming.

If you feel you're beyond reproach, inaccessible to bad people, or not likely to suffer a financial calamity, please read this chapter – twice. Early in my life, I felt fearless as my career and family began to build, only to be humbled by my own thoughtlessness, the unfortunate circumstances of others, and the rapidly evolving dynamics of life which can take everything away.

There are things you can do to reduce risk in your life to enhance your financial stability. This chapter highlights the primary potholes in the road for young Americans and offers proactive approaches to avoid jeopardy.

INSURING AGAINST RISK

Generally, people dislike paying for something they may never benefit from, like insurance. On the other hand, they dislike it a lot more when they lack insurance and lightning strikes. You can insure just about anything, yet you have to balance the cost against the benefits. At different points in your life, different types of insurance will be most worthwhile, so here's how I stack rank different forms of insurance for young Americans:

1. **Healthcare Insurance** may be a family benefit, government benefit, employer benefit, or you might buy it on an insurance exchange. I encourage you to get insured right away, then retain coverage continuously in order to access medical services as needed. Note that employees who are terminated from a job which provides health insurance have protection through "COBRA" and can maintain their benefits at a designated expense for eighteen months following termination in order to bridge to their next job's benefits.
2. **Dental Insurance** shares many characteristics with healthcare insurance. Overall healthcare is enhanced through oral health, as poor oral health creates problems for the body as well as the mouth. Because of this association, some policies offer both types of coverage.
3. **Auto Insurance** covers the repairs or replacement of a car or property you damage while driving your car. You can extend the "liability coverage" required by law with "comprehensive coverage" to insure your car as well. Many younger Americans acquire liability only, in the effort to save money given the costs of auto insurance and given their possibly poor driving records. If you can afford to replace your car with cash on hand, maybe you save money on the comprehensive insurance premium, but if not you should protect yourself with full coverage.

4. **Disability Insurance** pays you a portion of your regular employment income in the event you cannot work. This type of insurance can augment the disability benefits you may receive from Social Security in the event of a debilitating injury or illness.
5. **Homeowners insurance** covers the costs of repair or replacement of your home in the event of catastrophe. Generally, I'm not keen on Renters Insurance, unless your possessions are valuable and it would be catastrophic to lose them. Painful, sure. Catastrophic, maybe not, so the cost of the premium becomes debatable.
6. **Life Insurance** pays someone upon your death, thus becomes more relevant as others are dependent upon you. On your own, the merits are questionable and your money is better spent on building your estate and the other forms of insurance above.
7. **Umbrella Liability Coverage** protects you from a broad range of events, where the insurance types listed previously are deemed insufficient.

There are many other forms of insurance to address the needs of a wide variety of people and their unique situations. Generally, they are not relevant to a young American and you should save your money.

An Insurance Primer will help you shop for the best policies to fit your needs:

- The **Premium** is the amount you must pay for the insurance policy. The insurance companies have very complex formulas which help them determine the probability they'll have to pay out benefits. As with other concepts discussed in this book, low cost does not necessarily mean the best policy, as the following items determine value in concert with the cost/premium.
- The **Face Value/Coverage** is the dollar value or specific benefit the policy will pay upon a specific event occurring. The **Term** is how long the policy is in effect, providing coverage at the noted cost/premium.

- **The Deductible** is the amount of the expense you must pay before insurance begins paying benefits. For example, if you are in an auto accident which causes $1,500 in damages to your car and your deductible is $500, insurance will pay the repair company $1,000 for the repair of your car and you must pay the rest. Many people pay more for their insurance than they have to, as they insure with a low deductible, expecting the insurance company to pay for every little bill that may arise. As your financial capacity strengthens, I encourage higher deductibles, thus lower rates, depositing the difference in your savings account instead.

Shopping for insurance involves comparing policies from different providers and finding a good cost-benefit in a policy. Because of the broad range of young Americans' situations, I would be doing a disservice by suggesting how much coverage to purchase. Instead, my strong counsel is to purchase insurance in the order I outlined earlier, only purchasing additional forms of insurance if you determine your personal risks merit coverage. Select an excellent company rather than simply the lowest premium, and work with a representative/company you feel can continue to work with you as your life evolves. There are many companies who specialize in certain types of insurance, but as with financial institutions, I encourage you to consolidate your policies with fewer vendors, then every few years review coverage and costs, tweaking your policies and provider(s) accordingly.

I remember sitting in a theatre in 1993, watching Jurassic Park, as Steven Spielberg brought author Michael Crichton's creatures to life. With its incredible animation and creativity, most people were captivated by the reality. Most vivid for me were the scenes involving the raptors. Beyond their physical attributes, we saw the horror of their intellect at work, as they demonstrated their ability to learn human behaviors and correct their tactics while working in tandem with other raptors to kill their next meal.

Today, the raptors are more numerous, not limited by the bodies of water separating continents nor the trivial levels of security deployed by most people. Millions of individuals and many organized groups of people are working 24/7 to separate you from your money. They are tracking your keystrokes, monitoring your purchasing habits, sending you engaging emails and waiting for the right time to leverage all they have studied so they can **take you down.**

> ### Perspective:
> ### Cyber Security and Hackers
>
> 10/26/12 "Early last year, hackers were discovered embedding malicious software in two million computers, opening a virtual door for criminals to rifle through users' valuable personal and financial information. Last fall, an overseas crime ring was shut down after infecting four million computers, including half a million in the U.S. In recent months, some of the biggest companies and organizations in the U.S. have been working overtime to fend off continuous intrusion attacks aimed at their networks. The scope and enormity of the threat—not just to private industry but also to the country's heavily networked critical infrastructure—was spelled out last month in Director Robert S. Mueller's testimony to a Senate homeland security panel: **"Computer intrusions and network attacks are the greatest cyber threat to our national security."**
>
> Source: Federal Bureau of Investigation

Cybercrime is an epidemic for which we pay every day. Our costs include higher prices on products and services, higher taxation to pay for our protection, and institutional paralysis as leaders are paranoid about their organization's liability should something go wrong on their watch. The people who perpetuate the attacks are criminals who are wasting peoples' time and money.

What can you do when such advanced threats exist, to the point that our national security advisors are raising the alarm? As with every topic in this book, there are many things you can do to avoid attacks while also reducing the risk that you may propagate the threat by passing on the problems to those you communicate with.

- **Password protect** your devices and applications. Sure, it requires a few keystrokes every time you want to access something, but having used leading technology since the 80's, I know the sense of loss people get when their increasingly robust devices are lost along with hundreds of contact records, calendars, and other private data stored on them. You don't usually sense the hurt until it's too late. This is not something you want to experience. Change your passwords every 60-90 days and avoid overly simplistic passwords, such as the use of your birthday or name.
- **Firewall your computer** by installing leading virus protection software and subscribing to their automated updates, which are often available through your internet service provider. Such software programs filter and screen incoming communications, including emails, requests from remote system to connect to your systems and other such dastardly stuff. The proliferation of new strains of virus and Trojan horse programs requires us to stay one step ahead of the lowly criminals initiating the attacks. To miss this essential is like leaving your front open during a neighborhood crime wave.
- **Firewall your network** to keep out unwanted users. Connecting to the Internet has been improved with wireless routers, allowing multiple computers to piggyback the single connection through the wireless router sitting on a shelf somewhere in your home. The router can be password protected to reduce the risk of unwanted connections from people on the street in front of your home, or your neighbors. Only share the network access password with trusted family and friends, but never share your network administrative password.
- **Acquire certified software** from primary vendors. There are countless exciting programs for your phone, computer, and tablet which can do just about anything you want. Your desire to find the next great freeware app may come at a big price as you could load a "free" program that includes an embedded "Trojan horse", capable of doing terrible damage to your device and all of the devices yours interacts with. Rather than accept an unsolicited offer from anyone,

seek out applications on the trusted exchanges you know, run by vendors who vet the applications. Just because a web-site shows 5 stars on the advertisement and a bunch of bogus user-reviews does not mean you should download and test it. Once the raptors are in the kitchen, you're toast.

- **Don't nibble at the bait** by opening an email from someone you don't know, even unsolicited emails from major brands you think are innocuous. Avoid opening links embedded within emails, instead copying the web address into your browser if needed.

- **Trust your senses** as if you're ready to drink a glass of milk. If it smells off a bit, do you drink it anyway? Of course not. Same theory should apply to online offers, solicitations and "friends" who want to connect with you. Social networks have become diluted through excessive non-friend connections. Raptors mine people's data presented in cyberspace, building upon the instant familiarity to cut these weak calves from the herd. As such, limit your presentation of private data in public.

- **Reduce your transactional affairs** to vendors you trust, beyond the software applications noted above. Whether you're buying blue jeans, dog food, or technology, saving a few bucks online is not worth the pain of a breach in your security or privacy. Fewer vendors means fewer records of your private data in fewer databases around the world. Much better.

- **Use payment methods offering protections,** rather than sharing your banking data with any vendor. Various forms of digital currency are emerging, in addition to credit cards which have reasonable consumer protection baked into them. This acts as a form of financial account firewall, similar to the systems firewalls referenced earlier.

- **Don't use other peoples' systems to conduct business** or to access a password protected site. As easy as it is to connect here or there and do cool stuff online, you can't know if your friends or their guests are diligent in their security provisions. While they surely aren't interested in your affairs, they could have inadvertently loaded the keystroke logging program that some loser somewhere else is viewing as you enter your data. Same theory applies to public systems, for example at hotels, libraries, etc.

- **Automate bill payments** to reduce your need to login to do something which reoccurs regularly. This also takes a redundant task off of your list so you can focus your time elsewhere.

- **Backup your data each month,** using a password protected thumb drive, CD, or DVD, then store it off-site if possible. This protects you should your systems become compromised, by allowing you to restore a prior version of your files to a clean computer. Alternately, you can upload your files to a "cloud" storage service, but be sure to password protect the files using a certified zip file creation program.

We've all learned basic security provisions since childhood, but most of us were never taught the following:

- Only carry required items in your wallet, such as your driver's license, debit card, credit card, cash, etc. Securely store all unneeded personal identifying cards or financial cards for occasional use.

- Never provide your social security number over the phone, nor through the mail, even to an employer or presumed "safe" vendor. As this is your unique identifier it is prized by identity thieves who will then use it to access many other parts of your life.

- Retain receipts for all non-cash purchases, so you have a record of what you bought.

- Reconcile your financial accounts, matching your purchase receipts to online transactions weekly or to printed statements monthly.
By maintaining focus on this weekly or monthly, transaction remain familiar to you and you can catch errors and breaches in a timely way.

- Do not respond to phone calls or emails soliciting any information. If the communication appears legitimate, initiate a call to their number of record (not the one in their communication) and verify the need for information with their staff.

- Store sensitive personal and financial records in a portable safe or locked drawer at home, or use a safe deposit box at your financial institution. Because many young Americans' living situations change often, a safe deposit box provides a long-term secure place for private records. Similarly, establishing a PO Box for your mail reduces concerns for privacy in a shared mailbox and simplifies future changes in residence.
- Elect to receive bills and statements by email to eliminate paper records which can be mishandled somewhere between the sender and your mailbox.

Stuff happens. Because of the many trap doors in our systems and processes, there will come a time when your data is compromised. Here are the recommended steps to reducing collateral damage:

- **Immediately** report a compromise to the involved financial institutions, terminating a lost credit card for example, and ordering a new one.
- Monitor all transactions and related accounts daily, cooperating with financial institution(s) as needed
- Where identity theft is of concern, you may place a "freeze" on credit reporting with credit reporting agencies until issues are resolved, blocking new accounts from being formed in your name.
- Reflect upon what may have caused the breach. Take personal corrective action to reduce the chance of such problems in the future.

"I'm Agent John Johnson, with the IRS. I'd like to speak with you regarding your tax returns for the past 3 years. May I come in?"

TAX JEOPARDY

Let me tell you how it will be,
There's one for you, nineteen for me 'Cause I'm the taxman,
Yeah, I'm the taxman Should five percent appear too small,
Be thankful I don't take it all 'Cause I'm the taxman,

... The Beatles

George Harrison penned these lyrics in 1966, as money was rolling in for The Beatles, out of disgust for the 95% tax rate charged to high income citizens throughout Britain. But love 'em or hate 'em, you've gotta to pay 'em. Countries, states, counties and cities require tax revenues to provide the services their citizens demand.

Throughout my consulting career I've been surprised at the broad array of attitudes and emotions surrounding the topic of taxation; opinions differ regarding what taxes are spent on, how much should be spent, and who should pay the taxes. Feelings range from self-centered to idealistic, and I've learned that the emotions are so deeply seated that debate is counter-productive in a social or business setting. Yet, the debate rages on, as our country's gap between the wealthy and the poor increases in an unhealthy direction.

My wife and I have paid plenty of taxes, while shying away from speculative or questionable tax-planning strategies just to save a few bucks. I went to public K-12 schools, a public university (Oregon State University), and received benefits from tax dollars for various programs throughout my life. As a result I feel a commitment to contribute to the pie from which I ate for so long. That said, I lack confidence in how my hard earned tax dollars are being spent by the government, which I suspect is the root of most folks' gripes about taxation.

So, why are taxes a part of this Jeopardy chapter? Two reasons. First, people who don't understand taxes are less likely to file their taxes accurately and on time. Second, people who defy the system may have great reasoning, but are likely going to lose against a very big gorilla and pay stiff penalties as a result. The way to win is to learn the essentials, structure your affairs in a tax-efficient way and process your tax returns properly. Tax code is monstrous, with thousands of intricacies and inter-dependencies. Thus, to fill in one box on a tax form, you've got to reference boxes x and y first. That sort of fork in the road instantly loses half the crowd unnecessarily. Let's get familiar with the essentials, without feeling like we need to know it all. The personal taxes you can expect to pay early in your life are:

- **Income Taxes** are levied by federal, and some state and local agencies, who may tax as a portion of your income as they and/or their voters approve. Designated income may include payroll income, dividend and interest income, income from businesses, etc.
- **Sales Taxes** are common in nearly all states throughout the US, taxing all people on consumption of goods and some services. As people spend more money they will pay increased taxes based upon their presumed higher income or wealth levels as they consume higher value goods than people of lesser means.
- **Social Security taxes** are a payroll tax, which employees and employers must pay, based on each employee's compensation.
- **Property taxes** pay for services not covered by federal or state taxes. Such taxes are for home and land owners, based upon a calculation using property value owned by you, invoiced each year.
- **Specialized taxes** are implemented when a government entity seeks additional revenue for services, or where they want to persuade/ dissuade activities. Cigarettes, for example, carry a stiff premium because of the implicit healthcare costs and captive taxpayers. Or, a luxury tax may be applied to high-end purchases, as the taxing authority assumes the wealthy are buying the luxury items and can afford another tax-hit.

FILING TAX RETURNS

Certainty? In this world nothing is certain but death and taxes.

... Benjamin Franklin

Tax reporting and filing is usually an annual ritual which people both dread as it arrives and celebrate as it departs. In essence, you are required to tell the IRS (Federal and State) what you earned, where it came from, and what deductions you are claiming to reduce taxable earnings. Then, of course, you are telling the IRS what you owe them or they owe you. I like it when they owe me!

In Chapter 6, I recommended filling in your employment W4 in a conservative way, so your employer will withhold a little too much, rather than too little and creating a taxes-due situation at year-end. A refund is a wonderful thing.

Mid April is the filing deadline, meaning your returns must be post marked on or before that date, or your online filing must be accepted on or before that date. The reason people file on April 15th is because they don't love filing taxes and put things off until the last moment. Bad idea. You are more apt to make errors or file a late return. A good rule of thumb is to do your filing a month earlier, so if something arises you have that padding to assure things are done on time. In the event it's just not feasible to file your return by this deadline, you can file an extension to defer until mid October.

On-line filing is much easier than manual forms, using a variety of services and IRS resources. Millions of taxpayers now use popular computer software or the rapidly emerging class of cloud applications offered by tax processing companies. If your tax return simply involves entering information from your employer's W2 form, consider doing your tax filing yourself using a free online process found at http://www.irs.gov/uac/Free-File:-Do-Your-Federal-Taxes-for-Free.

If your tax situation involves more complex matters, my recommendation is to hire a **Registered Tax Return Preparer** or **CPA** (Certified Public Accountant) to assist you in your initial filings and familiarize yourself with the process. Sure, you'll pay a fee, but you'll be better able to file correctly and learn in the process. From there, you can choose to file on your own in the future, should you be interested in the process and feel technically competent. Consider that this task occurs only once per year, thus the likelihood of developing expertise is low. This is a good reason to seek help or oversight.

Speaking of tax payments, some of the wealthiest in our society have directed large portions of their wealth into non-profit foundations, in order to guide the impact of those dollars rather than turn them over to family or government upon their deaths. By gifting their assets to a charity, they reduce the size of their taxable estate and taxable income and thus pay less in taxes during their life and after.

The Gates, Buffets, and other such accomplished leaders recognize the importance of enhancing broad social missions to enhance life for all rather than a select few. This sort of wealth redistribution should increase in the coming years as other leaders come of age and build upon the examples of such visionaries.

I hate paying taxes. But I love the civilization they give me

... Oliver Wendell Holmes Sr.

HEALTH JEOPARDY is included in this book because of the cause and effect relationship between health and finance. Our capacity to earn a living and to save money is directly correlated with our physical and mental health, allowing us to seek a broader range of jobs, while reducing disruptions in pay and out of pocket medical expenses.

PERSPECTIVE: TAX DOLLARS AT WORK

- The U.S. spends 2.5 times more than the average country for healthcare, , yet performs well below many other countries in heart attack fatalities, infant mortality, and life expectancy.
- The obesity rate among adults was 36.5 % in 2011, up from 15% in 1978. The US has the highest rate among OECD countries. Obesity's growing prevalence foreshadows increases in the occurrence of health problems (such as diabetes and cardiovascular diseases), and higher health care costs in the future.

SOURCE: ORGANISATION FOR ECONOMIC COOPERATION AND DEVELOPMENT

When you think about excellent physical health, you may envision a buffed out hard body, yet as with all things we get back to balance. Maintaining a ritual of cardiovascular exercise will deter many health demons, whether you choose walking or a more rigorous routine. Weaving weight-bearing exercises into your routine will reduce the risk of injury from common daily accidents, simply due to improved core strength. Again, we're not talking Superhero here, as three 45 minute sessions a week can help you to hold the line on health. Such a routine fills time and reduces out of pocket expenses people would otherwise experience from couch potato activities.

A healthy diet compliments exercise, yet does not have to be financially painful. Interestingly, better food can save you money. Dr Oz, through his shows, web-site and interviews, has demonstrated many methods to reduce intake of the wrong stuff and stock your kitchens with the right stuff for less money. Too often, people shop for food non-strategically, wandering the isles and grabbing stuff. Going in the store with a shopping list will keep your budget and your health on track.

Let's move onto a dimension of health many people are uncomfortable discussing. Millions in our country are in great physical health yet suffer from mental health disorders. Such disorders are often caused by genetics, substance abuse, physical abuse, mental abuse, and breakdowns in our social systems. That's the bad news. The good news is that most such syndromes are treatable. So what does this have to do with money?

Approximately 26% of adults suffer from some form of mental illness and it is the leading cause of disability in America. For example, as you read this, millions of millennials could instantly break into a cold sweat if certain events occur in certain settings in their daily lives, as a result of their anxiety disorder. The events trigger an avalanche of defensive reactions and disallow the coping mechanisms others take for granted. They avoid many aspects of daily life, therefore reducing their fulfillment, productivity and financial capacity. Add depression, bipolar disorder, and other maladies to anxiety and you surely will encounter many such people unknowingly in your typical day.

Those who have access to counseling can learn techniques to build coping skills to allow full participation in society. Such treatment usually goes well beyond medications, as effective behavioral therapies have emerged to reduce the dependence upon drugs.

Mental health's stigma is changing for the better, as we are learning that disorders can happen to anyone and that our world is full of incredible people who are often being held back by a treatable condition. Proactive treatment can reduce the pain and damage a disorder may cause in financial stability, work and personal relationships.

BEHAVIORAL JEOPARDY occurs from controllable events, activities and choices we each make each day. Early in my adulthood, a leader I respected pulled me aside and asked me why I still partied with the crowd. I explained my reasoning and admitted that there were times the party won, but I didn't. He laughed at some of the stories, then explained some of his sad experiences earlier in his life. He went on to say "When I drink, I don't always make big mistakes, but when I make big mistakes, I've always been drinking." At that moment something sunk in for me, as I'd felt what he was describing. At a point, each of us must decide whether we are willing to risk it all through our behavioral choices, or hang out with people who are inclined to do so.

Drugs and Alcohol are pervasive, yet the "liability of libations" has such immense proof of danger we shouldn't need any more convincing. But apparently we need convincing. It has gotten so bad that employers now report that they struggle filling many jobs because qualified candidates fail their drug tests or have suspended driver's licenses resulting from drinking and driving.

Driving is so elementary in most people's lives and important for so many careers that you'd think safe driving is a no-brainer. But between DUI's, speeding tickets, and accidents caused by multi-tasking, courts around the country are losing tolerance; large fines along with time behind bars has become routine. The effect on personal finances comes from fines, higher insurance costs, and employment limitations.

Violence, Theft and Property Damage are prevalent in our society. For example, The National Coalition Against Domestic Violence reports that an estimated 1.3 million women are victims of physical assault by an intimate partner each year. Females who are 20-24 years of age are at the greatest risk of nonfatal intimate partner violence. For each victim, there is a perpetrator and both lose.

Gambling has moved from a very controlled and limited vice to a plague which feeds on all types in our society. With various states getting in the act to garner tax revenues, gambling has essentially been certified by regional governments. The personal risk is thus magnified by gambling's presence within communities and online sites, no longer requiring a plane trip somewhere else.

19th century writer Ambrose Bierce wrote, "A lottery is a tax on people who are bad at math". As people's finances fall into disarray due to gambling addictions, the balance of their lives collapse as well.

So why is all this stuff still happening, when the negative outcomes are so obvious?

Guilt by association - Most people don't invent bad ideas, nor harmful actions, yet fall into bad stuff because of who they are hanging out with. You may be envisioning drug dealers, gangs and really sketchy stuff, but it comes all the way down to other peoples' values and fundamental choices which are inconsistent with yours. You become what you surround yourself with. Being in the wrong place at the wrong time sounds like a matter of bad luck, but when you think about the time of day, the type of place, the activities going on, and the people who will be there, you can do some rough probability analysis without pulling out your calculator.

An Idle Mind Is the Devil's Playground - Our world has become more insular with technology and the plethora of lousy media being shovelled into our living rooms. The resulting lack of socialization and dumbing down old fashioned interactivity creates a void, making people susceptible to bad ideas and bad associations. By building a life which revolves around your values and objectives, you naturally get busy with stuff which narrows the opportunities to get into trouble.

Desperation and Greed - Many people who suffer setbacks or have overly ambitious and self-centered goals, attempt to fill the gaps by cheating others and cutting required corners. Financial success is built through a long period of good habits, hard work, and service to others. Win/win works, win/lose doesn't, as the world ultimately catches up with people who are not fair in their arrangements with others. Beyond your own behaviors, constantly assess others for signs of greed or desperation and choose your company wisely.

> Let me ask you one question, Is your money that good
> Will it buy you forgiveness, Do you think that it could
> I think you will find, When your death takes its toll
> All the money you made, Will never buy back your soul
>
> ... Bob Dylan

ESTATE JEOPARDY arises when people become incapacitated or die, but lack directions for their healthcare and the care of their family or finances. If you are dazed (after reading this book) and walk out on the street and are hit by a bus, two things are likely. You'll either leave this earth as you know it, or be unable to care for yourself, including decisions about your money or healthcare, or care for loved ones you may leave behind.

Who will decide what to do for you, or what to do with your resources, or care for your children? Maybe your designated loved ones can step in, if they were not hit by the same bus? A government representative or court? What if everyone disagrees? Is that really the way we want to leave things? Usually, the answer is no, yet estate planning is a touchy and uncomfortable topic so it is often not addressed in advance of problems. As with all things in this book, let's break it down to the essential ingredients and outline some simple steps you can take as you age to build the appropriate mechanisms for clarity and comfort. Also, consider that these concepts apply just as much to your parents and siblings and there may come a time for you to assure they have attended to these matters as well.

A **Durable Power of Attorney** allows you to designate people to make financial decisions and access your financial accounts should you be unable to do so because of injury or illness ("incapacity").

Advanced Directives address healthcare decisions during your incapacity: A) A Healthcare Power of Attorney, or otherwise known as a Healthcare "Proxy" allows people you designate to make health care decisions on your behalf should you become incapacitated. B) A Living Will defines your preferences, regarding your medical care during incapacity and whether to prolong your life. Such directives reduce the stress on loved ones, who may otherwise struggle with such decisions if they don't know your preferences.

A **Will** defines how your estate will distribute upon your passing, who the guardians for your minor children will be and in some cases creates a trust.

A **Trust** can govern the care of your estate during incapacity, and may live on beyond your passing - unlike a Will's termination at death. For many families, a trust helps deceased parents protect monies from outright distributions to younger children, or to accomplish very specific business and estate objectives. For those who become incapacitated through aging, injury or disease, a trust defines who will manage specific aspects of their financial affairs ("trustee") and any related preferences or directions. While trusts are beyond most young Americans' needs, as you build a family and wealth just know that such capabilities exist; trusts are not reserved for billionaires and will be worthy of your review with your attorney at a future point.

If you are tight on funds and not willing to pay someone to help you, you can download forms from an accredited web-site within your state and prepare rudimentary documents (find helpful links in bibliography and resources guide). Otherwise, I encourage you to seek out an attorney who can create the needed legal documents to best assure your expectations are honored if the unthinkable occurs. While you can try to interpret the complexities of such documents, this is one of those tasks you'll want handled properly. Short of engaging the attorney and spending money on their time and expertise, get a grip on some things in advance:

- **Who** do you want to get **what** from your estate (mementos, savings, car, etc)?
- Download a copy of your state's approved Advanced Healthcare Directive/Living Will and prepare draft responses to the questionnaire, as these highly personal healthcare decisions are less influenced by an attorney.
- Who do you want to be responsible for serving as your Healthcare Power of Attorney and Financial (durable) Power of Attorney?
- If you have kids, who do you want to care for them and what specific requests would you make of the guardians?

Last, I encourage you to sign/execute the documents upon completion, store a copy with the attorney or family member and securely file a copy for your reference, including possibly notifying key participants to their possible future duties. Every three years, review them to determine if you should revisit the process with an attorney to assure the documents are effective.

YOUR FORTRESS

We all need help.
Professionals can help us navigate the maze of life, yet we must be able to afford their help. There are many government and non-profit agencies which provide support to Americans of limited means. Whether you are establishing paid or complimentary arrangements, following are the experts I encourage you to engage as your needs evolve in your early adult years.

- **Doctor and Dentist** - By building relationships early, medical professionals are able to offer guidance in consideration of your history. Also, as medical professionals are expected to be in demand, you'll be able to secure appointments with preferred professionals rather than be declined. Leverage low cost clinics for common colds and such, if the access or expense of seeing your doctor is prohibitive.
- **Financial Planner** - As you get your feet on the ground with your career and initial savings, a Certified Financial Planner (CFP®) can help you chart a course which is very specific to you, beyond my generalizations in this book.
- **Insurance Agent** - Someone who can provide you with advice on policies, without selling you more insurance than you need or can afford.
- **CPA or Registered Tax Return Preparer** - If your needs are straightforward and you still want help with your taxes, the Registered Tax Return Preparer can help you file your taxes and represent you should a conflict arise with the IRS. CPAs can extend this capability with a broad range of strategic counsel and a deeper technical capacity.
- **Attorney** - When ready to place a checkmark on the estate planning to-do list, find an attorney with such expertise, whose process you understand, and whose bills are within your budget.

- **Banker** - Although banking has become incredibly automated and structured for self-service, it's good to get to know a tenured person at your local branch should you seek guidance beyond standard banking matters. They can then refer you to mortgage specialists, investment specialists and many other associates or 3rd parties given their familiarity with comparable clients' needs and your community.
- **Investment Advisor** - An Investment Advisor or Broker can assist you in opening an account and investing monies. If you prefer self-managing your investments, using one of the approaches referenced in Chapter 9, such professionals will generally lack time for you as they earn their living serving longer term clients who pay them fees.
- **Real-estate Agent** - Whether renting or buying, an Agent offers expertise relative to specific neighborhoods and property types.

Here's my recommended approach to selecting an advisor:

- **Technical fit** - Titles and acronyms aside, do they know what they're talking about? Credentials? Experience with clients like you?
- **Personal fit** - Is this someone you will enjoy working with and would be comfortable calling to ask questions or discuss issues?
- **Company fit** - Does their company offer additional resources and do they have a solid reputation?
- **Additional capabilities** - Beyond what you are initially interested in, how else might they or their teammates help in the future?
- **Stability** - Most people do not want to re-explain all of their personal affairs every time a professional turns over. What is the likelihood this professional will continue to do this job for this company?
- **Pricing** - Levitt and Dubner's *Freakanomics* notes that "...experts are human, and humans respond to incentives. How any human treats you therefore, will depend on how that expert's incentives

are setup." Do you understand what the advisor will deliver, for what cost, given the criteria above?

Such professionals are presumably part of a state-wide professional association, and their companies are possibly screened by the Better Business Bureau. Thus, online lists are one approach to identifying candidates but getting professional referrals from friends and other professionals is a better approach. Then, do your due-diligence per the checklist above to assure a fit for you. You know the first three letters of assume.

No one cares about your money more than you, so I encourage you to stay close to the topics, while leveraging experts for oversight and technical help when it is needed. All of this stuff is overwhelming for most young Americans early in their lives, so you should know you're not alone if you feel that way. As with other concepts in this book, advisors can be added incrementally, as your needs, time and budget allow. See the Resources Guide at the back of this book for ideas.

Reducing the prospects of jeopardy and failure is a worthy objective, but we all fall down. Struggle is a fact of life and as we'll see in the next chapter, it can be one of the best things that happens to us, if we capitalize on the lessons learned.

CHAPTER 13

The Power of Struggle

The Power Of Struggle

The world loves to celebrate success. The images of highly successful people are all around us. But such images only tell part of their story and are usually focused on their accomplishment of the moment. Buried are the deals gone wrong, the personal tragedies, and the mistakes along the way.

What's most interesting in consulting with successful people is learning about their journey. What speed bumps did they hit and which wrong turns did they take? How did they get back on track? Who helped them along the way? If they could do it all over again, what would they do differently?

After interviewing thousands of successful and diverse people, across multiple industries and regions, a recurring theme emerged: struggles and the school of hard knocks are required ingredients for most success stories. Most successful people will gladly acknowledge "what went wrong" as they realize it is an important theme for the next generation of achievers..

The best of the best, in all industries, sports, academic and artistic endeavors, had their bumps and bruises many times over before their greatest accomplishments. Their struggles made them better and were not limited to difficult financial circumstances, as people wish they could reverse career choices, relationship choices, and personal decisions. But in the end, their success habits surpassed the failure factors and they broke through. This chapter summarizes such success habits, which will help you break through failures and struggles.

> You may encounter many defeats, but you must not be defeated.
> In fact, it may be necessary to encounter the defeats,
> so you can know who you are, what you can rise from,
> how you can still come out of it.
>
> *... Maya Angelou*

The gate to achievement - The fear of failure can be a positive driver or an inhibitor, depending on your orientation. I can't stand the idea of failing and it drives me to greater effort. It is easy to put my heart into something I believe in, but there is only so much heart to spread around. Every "opportunity", from community, to family, to corporate initiatives feels achievable to me and I can rationalize the sense of purpose. It is easy for me to get wrapped up in something. But unhealthy to get wrapped up in everything.

I leverage my fear of failure by committing "all in" to projects or efforts, stating a date of completion, an outcome, and whatever else makes sense. Then I march to that drumbeat every day, accomplishing my commitments a high percentage of the time, across multiple disciplines, in a variety of roles. Fact is, I'm not a genius at anything, but have learned that if I try and apply my lessons from past experiences, I can figure almost anything out. Balanced with a drive to deliver results, it's a recipe that works for me.

> It's kind of fun to do the impossible.
>
> ... Walt Disney

Many people don't sign up for challenging engagements, accepting routine roles in order to avoid any personal risk. That's usually driven by their concern for being branded a failure, or wasting their time on something they're not confident in. The opportunity to learn from struggles and to broaden capabilities is lost on such fear. Although much of life loads us up with unexciting tasks, avoiding stretching from time to time is a missed opportunity. I'm not talking about world records, just going a bit beyond your comfort zone to grow a little bit along the way.

As Malcolm Gladwell so clearly demonstrated in his book Outliers, mastery requires repetition and depth of knowledge that only comes through repeated experiences, extreme focus and a bit of good fortune. Imagine you make a commitment to try, fail, assess, improve, and try again. Try, fail, assess, improve, and try again. There is no shame.

This pattern builds new skills, but more importantly it builds confidence and potential mastery. In turn, mastery increases confidence, and the cycle repeats. It is an incredible feeling.

How do the pros deal with failure? - When the professional baseball player swings at a pitch, the ball is travelling so fast that freeze frame on an HDTV barely captures the moment the ball crosses the plate. You realize the masterful coordination of all dimensions of the athlete in connecting the bat with the ball. Consider that they have seen thousands of pitches, studied the pitchers hand movements and posture on game film and spent countless hours in the batting cage. They have a batting coach. Still, the best career batting average ever for a professional baseball player is .366, set by Ty Cobb in 1928. That means more than 6 out of 10 times he stepped up to the plate he did not get a hit and no player since him has done better.

Most people can barely handle failure in private. Can you imagine "failing" at your job in public 60% of the time? The thrill of victory overrides professionals' fear of failure, as they focus on success and know that struggle is part of the game. Entertainers and athletes are particularly impressive because of their mastery of their art, coupled with their courage to struggle on a public stage with competitors and distractions in their face. They are revered for a reason.

Yet, give yourself some credit. What the athlete is experiencing on the public stage is a flavor of what you deal with every day. Consider that time does not stand still, and others are constantly in attack mode as referenced throughout this book. You've got a lot to accomplish just to survive, right? Build upon your smaller victories, reminding yourself from time to time that everyone fails and people who succeed keep trying.

The struggles we experience can provide another layer of expertise and perspective which become invaluable battling the next challenge. There are specific traits which will help all people increase their probability for success, in spite of the struggles of a crummy economy or a unique personal dilemma. Let's walk through what you can do to break through tough times.

> "The greatest glory in living is not in never failing,
> but rising every time we fail."
>
> ... *Nelson Mandela*

SUCCESS TRAITS

You may determine that you'll never be a big shot leader of anything, but will be glad to be in the background living the life you love. Or, you may be driven to great accomplishments, as a social or business visionary, rallying others in your passion and driving change in a big, big way. It takes all kinds for our world to work and each of us must determine how to get the most out of what we've been given. All young Americans can all deploy the strategies I've laid out in this book to create a life of financial security and capacity to do many things. Here are the success traits which will serve you in financial matters and in life.

- **Crawl-walk-run** - Don't feel like you're supposed to be something grand on day one. You're not. Learn, try, improve, reset; learn, try, improve, reset. Most people who accomplish grand things do so through repeated effort and don't allow fear of failure to dissuade them.
- **Adapt -** The big power play for the coming years will be your ability to flex your approach and orientation as the world around you changes. As Tim Harford argues in his aptly named book *Adapt* people have historically looked to leaders for direction, yet the increasing unpredictability of our world requires individuals to be self-directed in response to change.
- **Constant entrepreneurism -** Imagine that the company is yours. What would you be doing to improve client satisfaction, product quality, process efficiency, profitability, etc? Successful entrepreneurs are active participants, not passive bystanders.

- **Empathy** - Effectiveness grows through empathy. By thinking through the eyes of the customer, owner, investor, supplier, teammate or other recipient, your actions will be more meaningful.
- **Balance** - Thousands of people I've advised have hit financial home runs, with ample resources to live comfortably the rest of their lives. They don't look back and say "I wish I'd made more money and not gone to my kids' games." The happiest people are those who find life balance along the way.
- **Humility** - Arrogance is both off-putting and destructive to the team and collaboration requirements noted in earlier chapters. A little swagger from time to time on a particular capability or achievement is ok, yet, generally the more you swagger the farther you distance yourself from others. Believe in yourself, but stay humble to assure you're open to new possibilities beyond your own "genius", to stay aligned with the rest of the human race.
- **Integrity** - People want to be associated with others they trust. Do onto others, as you would have them do onto you.
- **Patience** - Steady, disciplined decision making allows you to avoid being rushed into bad decisions. Opportunities are rarely so good you have to "act now or lose out". Time is on the side of the negotiator, so patience is a virtue you want to own.
- **Effort aligned with goals** - Effort is foundational to success. As Grant Cardone asserts in *THE 10X RULE*, extreme effort coupled with grand goals is something all of us can put to work in our daily lives to accomplish fantastic things.
- **Perseverance** - Mastery requires repetition. Survival requires hope. Success builds on both to push through situations with confidence, knowing that repetition and positive outlooks will carry the day.

I find that the harder I work, the more luck I seem to have.

... Thomas Jefferson

The concepts throughout this book can be applied to individuals, corporations, communities and governments. *The only way to assure financial freedom* is to:

1) engage in a regular planning process
2) periodically revise your plan to reflect situational and economic changes
3) modify strategies and behaviors as needed

Essentially, *you can't spend what you don't have, and you should own far more than you owe.*

Your next ten years will present an array of exciting opportunities and some scary situations which will test your success traits. Although this book doesn't engineer jobs or eliminate the pains which surely will confront all of us, my hope is that it makes your journey more enjoyable.

America continues to be the land of hope and opportunity for all. It's absolutely clear to me that your future is quite promising. Have fun along the way.

Paul

BIBLIOGRAPHY

Chapter 1 – You, Inc.

Naisbitt, John. *Megatrends: Ten New Directions Transforming Our Lives.* New York: Warner Books, 1982. Print.

Millennials: Confident. Connected. Open to Change. Pew Research. 10 February 2010. Web. Retrieved 12 August 2013. www.pewsocialtrends.org/2010/02/24/millennials-confident-connected-open-to-change/

Chapter 2 – Reality

Arnold, Chris. (2011). *How Technology is Eliminating Higher-Skill Jobs.* National Public Radio. 3 November 2011. Web. Retrieved 1 June 2013. www.npr.org/2011/11/03/141949820/how-technology-is-eliminating-higher-skill-jobs

Bruner, Jon. (2011). *U.S. Manufacturing Surges Ahead – But Don't Look For a Factory Job.* Forbes. 22 August 2011. Web. Retrieved 25 May 2013. www.forbes.com/sites/jonbruner/2011/08/22/u-s-manufacturing-surges-ahead-but-dont-look-for-a-factory-job-infographic/

Education and Employment. Crandall, Pierce & Company. http://www.crandallpierce.com

Chapter 3 – Renewal

Bor, D., Himmelstein, D., McCormick, D., Woolhander, S., Zallman, L. (2013). *Immigrants Contributed An Estimated $115.2 Billion More To The Medicare Trust Fund Than They Took Out In 2002 -09.* Health Affairs, 32:6 (1153-1160) http://content.healthaffairs.org/content/early/2013/05/20/hlthaff.2012.1223.full.html

Carnevale, A. P., Smith, N., Strohl, J. (2013). *Recovery: Job Growth and Education Requirements Through 2020.* Georgetown Public Policy Institute: Center on Education and the Workforce. http://cew.georgetown.edu/recovery2020/

Naim, Moisés. *The End of Power.* New York: Basic Books. 2013, Print.

Sightings, Tom. (2013). *How Baby-Boomers Will Change the Economy.* USA News. 15 January 2013. Web. Retrieved 19 March 2013. http://money.usnews.com/money/blogs/On-Retirement/2013/01/15/how-baby-boomers-will-change-the-economy

Simon, Stephanie. (2013). *High School Graduation Rate Up Sharply, But Red Flags Abound.* Rueters. 25 February 2013. Web. Retrieved 7 June 2013. http://www.reuters.com/article/2013/02/25/us-highschool-idUSBRE91O0JY20130225

Toossi, Mitra. (2012). *Labor Force Projections to 2020: A More Slowly Growing Workforce.* Bureau of Labor Statistics. 21 February 2012. Web. Retrieved 17 May 2013. http://www.bls.gov/opub/mlr/2012/01/art3full.pdf

GDP (Current US$). The World Bank. 12 June 2013. Web. Retrieved 12 June 2013. www.data.worldbank.org/indicator/NY.GDP.MKTP.CD

The Next Decade in Global Wealth Among Millionaire Households: Highlights From a Study Conducted by the Deloitte Center for Financial Services. (2011). Retrieved 08 June 2013. https://www.deloitte.com/assets/Dcom-UnitedStates/Local%20Assets/Documents/FSI/US_FSI_GlobalWealthExecutiveSummary_050611.pdf

Where US Energy is Produced: An Interactive Map. NBC News. 5 May 2011. Web. Retrieved 4 June 2013. http://www.nbcnews.com/id/51181011

Chapter 4 – Finding A Job

Lockard, C.B., Wolf, Michael. (2012). *Occupational Employment Projections to 2020.* Bureau of Labor Statistics. January 2012. Web. Retrieved 5 March 2013. http://www.bls.gov/opub/mlr/2012/01/art5full.pdf

Pozin, Ilya. (2012). *How to Avoid Being a Startup Failure.* Forbes. 28 November 2012. Web. Retrieved 2 June 2013. http://www.forbes.com/sites/ilyapozin/2012/11/28/how-to-avoid-being-a-startup-failure/

Toossi, Mitra. (2012). *Projections of the labor force to 2050: A Visual Essay.* Bureau of Labor Statistics. 14 October 2012. Web. Retrieved 24 March 2013. http://www.bls.gov/opub/mlr/2012/10/art1full.pdf

30 Year Fixed-Rate Mortgages Since 1971. http://www.freddiemac.com/pmms/pmms30.htm

Small business stats, facts and tools, http://www.sba.gov/

Survey: 34 Percent of Firms to Add Temporary Workers. Aerotek. 6 April 2012. Web. Retrieved 23 May 2013. http://www.aerotek.com/about-aerotek/staffing-news/survey-34-percent-of-firms-to-add-temporary-workers/97

Websters Dictionary. http://www.merriam-webster.com/dictionary/indispensable

Chapter 5 – Protecting A Job

10 Rules that Govern Groups: What Most People Have in Common. PsyBlog. Retrieved 12 June 2013. http://www.spring.org.uk/2009/07/10-rules-that-govern-groups.php

Chapter 6 – Who Wins The Race?

Browne, Andrea N. (2012). *Frugal Habits of the Super Rich.* Kiplinger. 5 July 2012. Web. Retrieved 7 June 2013. http://www.kiplinger.com/slideshow/spending/T037-S001-frugal-habits-of-the-super-rich/index.html

Kahneman, Daniel. *Thinking, Fast and Slow.* New York: Farrar, Straus & Giroux. 2013, Print.

http://money.cnn.com/calculator/pf/cost-of-living/

http://www.bestplaces.net/cost-of-living/

http://www.payscale.com/cost-of-living-calculator

Chapter 7 – Pick Any Door

Brown, M., Donghood, L., Klaauw, W.V.D., Mabutas, M.. (2012). *Grading Student Loans.* Federal Reserve Bank of New York. 5 March 2012. Web. Retrieved 8 April 2013. http://libertystreeteconomics.newyorkfed.org/2012/03/grading-student-loans.html?utm_source=feedburner&utm_medium=feed&utm_campaign=Feed%3A+LibertyStreetEconomics+%28Liberty+Street+Economics%292DeSilver,

Drew. (2013). *In Time for Graduation Season, a Look at Student Debt.* Pew Research. 13 May 2013. Web. Retrieved 20 May 2013. http://www.pewresearch.org/fact-tank/2013/05/13/in-time-for-graduation-season-a-look-at-student-debt/

Free Credit Reports: Information. Federal Trade Commission: Consumer Information. 5 March 2013. Web. Retrieved 20 March 2013. http://www.consumer.ftc.gov/articles/0155-free-credit-reports

Chapter 8 – Tradeoffs / Saving

Aridas, T., Pasquali, V., (2012). *Household Savings Rates.* Global Finance Magazine. 5 June 2012. Web. Retrieved 8 June 2013. http://www.gfmag.com/tools/global-database/economic-data/12065-household-saving-rates.html#ixzz2YgrC44Z5

Kadlec, Dan. (2012). *How a Digital Picture of Your Future Self Can Change Your Saving Habits.* Time. 29 February 2012. Web. Retrieved 1 June 2013. http://business.time.com/2012/02/29/how-a-digital-picture-of-your-future-self-can-change-your-saving-habits/

Schepp, David. (2012). *Boomers Retiring Earlier Than Expected, Cite Bad Health, Job Loss.* AOL Jobs. 4 April 2012. Web. Retrieved 2 June 2013. http://jobs.aol.com/articles/2012/04/04/boomers-retiring-earlier-than-expected-due-to-bad-health-job-lo/

Wiatrowski, William J. (2011). *Changing Landscape of Employment-Based Retirement Benefits.* Bureau of Labor Statistics. 29 September 2011. Web. Retrieved 4 May 2013. http://www.bls.gov/opub/cwc/cm20110927ar01p1.htm

Personal Savings Rates & trends http://research.stlouisfed.org/fred2/series/PSAVERT/

Social Security Basic Facts. The U.S. Social Security Administration. 19 June 2013. Web. Retrieved 1 July 2013. http://www.ssa.gov/pressoffice/basicfact.htm

Social Security - Average Monthly Benefit. http://ssa-custhelp.ssa.gov/app/answers/detail/a_id/13/~/average-monthly-social-security-benefit-for-a-retired-worker

Chapter 9 – The Investment Carnival

Olen, Helaine. *Pound Foolish.* New York, Penguin Publishing. 2012, Print.

The Effect of Inflation: Asset Allocation Risk and Reward. Crandall, Pierce & Company. http://www.crandallpierce.com

Chapter 10 – It's Complicated

Wang, Wendy. (2013). *For Young Adults, the Ideal Marriage Meets Reality.* Pew Research. 10 July 2013. Web. Retrieved 11 July 2013. http://www.pewresearch.org/fact-tank/2013/07/10/for-young-adults-the-ideal-marriage-meets-reality/

Chapter 11 – Beyond You

Charitable Institution Analysis. Better Business Bureau. Web. Retrieved 28 June 2013. http://www.bbb.org/us/charity-reviews

Chronicle of small good deeds done by individuals around US. http://www.npr.org/blogs/participationnation/2012/09/01/160328858/americans-in-action-helping-each-other-and-making-the-whole-country-better

Benefits of Volunteering. World Volunteer Web: Volunteerism Worldwide. 19 October 2005. Web. Retrieved 2 June 2013. http://www.worldvolunteerweb.org/resources/how-to-guides/volunteer/doc/benefits-of-volunteering.html

Millennial Impact Report. January 2012. Web. Retrieved 12 May 2013. http://cdn.trustedpartner.com/docs/library/AchieveMCON2013/Infographs.pdf

Oregon Attorney General's 20 Worst Charities: 2012. Deptartment of Justice: Oregon. Web. Retrieved 6 June 2013. http://www.doj.state.or.us/charigroup/pdf/attorney_generals_20_worst_charities_2012.pdf

Chapter 12 – Jeopardy

America's Drug Use Profile: Consequences of Illegal Drug Use. Office of National Drug Control Policy. Web. Retrieved 5 March 2013. https://www.ncjrs.gov/ondcppubs/publications/policy/99ndcs/ii-b.html

COBRA Continuation Health Coverage. The United States Department of Labor. Web. Retrieved 15 June 2013. http://www.dol.gov/ebsa/faqs/faq-consumer-cobra.html

Cyber Security: Focusing on Hackers and Intrusions. Federal Bureau of Investigations. 26 October 2012. Web. Retrieved 4 May 2013. http://www.fbi.gov/news/stories/2012/october/cyber-division-focusing-on-hackers-and-intrusions

Dr. Mehmet Oz. Health Splurges That Will Save You Money. The Dr. Oz Show. 13 May 2013. Web. Retrieved 7 June 2013. http://www.doctoroz.com/videos/health-splurges-save-you-money

Domestic Violence Facts. The National Coalition Against Domestic Violence. Retreived 10 June 2013. http://www.ncadv.org/files/DomesticViolenceFactSheet%28National%29.pdf

Key Findings: United States. Health at a Glance 2011: OECD Indicators. October 2011. Web. Retrieved 10 May 2013. http://www.oecd.org/els/health-systems/49084319.pdf

Germanotta, C., Ross, R. (2013). *A Kinder, Braver Mental Health World.* Huffington Post. 3 June 2013. Web. Retrieved 5 June 2013. http://www.huffingtonpost.com/cynthia-germanotta/a-kinder-braver-mental-health-world_b_3381158.html

How to Choose a Financial Planner. The Wall Street Journal. http://guides.wsj.com/personal-finance/managing-your-money/how-to-choose-a-financial-planner/

Insurance policy and company selection. http://www.usa.gov/topics/money/insurance/tips.shtml

What is Anxiety Disorder? National Institute of Mental Health. Web. Retrieved 28 April 2013. http://www.nimh.nih.gov/health/topics/anxiety-disorders/index.shtml

Chapter 13 – Jeopardy

MLB Career Batting Leaders. ESPN. Retrieved 22 August 2013 from http://espn.go.com/mlb/history/leaders

Gladwell, Malcolm. *Outliers: The Story of Success.* New York: Little Brown. 2008, Print.

Cardone, Grant. *The 10X Rule.* Hoboken: John Wiley & Sons. 2011, Print.

Harford, Tim. *Adapt.* New York: Picador. 2011, Print.

Samson, Anthony. *Mandela: The Authorized Biography.* Vintage. 2000, Print.

RESOURCES GUIDE

Economic data and trends

Ayres, Sarah. (2013). *America's 10 Million Unemployed Youth Spell Danger for Future Economic Growth.* June 2013. Web Retrieved 4 September 2013.

Brown, M., Donghood, L., Klaauw, W.V.D., Mabutas, M. (2012). *Grading Student Loans.* Federal Reserve Bank of New York. 5 March 2012. Web. Retrieved 8 April 2013. http://libertystreeteconomics.newyorkfed.org/2012/03/grading-student-loans.html?utm_source=feedburner&utm_medium=feed&utm_campaign=Feed%3A+LibertyStreetEconomics+%28Liberty+Street+Economics%292

Casselman, Ben. (2013). *Real Culprit Behind Smaller Workforce: Age.* The Wall Street Journal. 29 April 2013. Web. Retrieved 5 June 2013. http://online.wsj.com/article/SB10001424127887323798104578450651084576338.html

The Huffington Post. Posted: 04/22/2013. 16 Iconic American Companies Founded By Immigrants. http://www.huffingtonpost.com/2013/04/22/american-companies-founded-by-immigrants_n_3116172.html

Lowrie, Annie. (2013). *Wealth Gap Among Races Has Widened Since Recession.* New York Times. 28 April 2013. Web. Retrieved 10 June 2013. http://www.nytimes.com/2013/04/29/business/racial-wealth-gap-widened-during-recession.html?pagewanted=all&_r=0

Sightings, Tom. (2013). *How Baby-Boomers Will Change the Economy.* USA News. 15 January 2013. Web. Retrieved 19 March 2013. http://money.usnews.com/money/blogs/On-Retirement/2013/01/15/how-baby-boomers-will-change-the-economy

Personal brand development

DeLisser, Peter. *Be Your Own Executive Coach: Master High Impact Communications Skills for: Dealing With Difficult People, Improving Your Personal Image, Learning How to Listen and Solving Business Problems Creatively.* Worcester: Chandler House Press. 1999, Print.

Kerzner, Harold R. *Project Management: A Systems Approach to Planning, Scheduling, and Controlling, 11th Edition.* Somerset: Wiley Publishing, 2013, Print.

Richmond, Emily. (2013). *High School Graduation Rate Hits 40-Year Peak in the U.S.* The Atlantic. 6 June 2013. Web. Retrieved 1 August 2013. http://www.theatlantic.com/national/archive/2013/06/high-school-graduation-rate-hits-40-year-peak-in-the-us/276604/

Sparks, Sarah D. (2013). *A "Neglected" Population Gets Another Chance at a Diploma.* Education Week. 31 May 2013. Web. Retrieved 1 August 2013. http://www.edweek.org/ew/articles/2013/06/06/34overview.h32.html?intc=EW-DC13-TOC

Employment

Bennett, John. (2013). *Mayor of "Food Stamp Town" Fights Back.* Human Events. 16 May 2013. Web. Retrieved 6 June 2013. http://www.humanevents.com/2013/05/16/governor-of-food-stamp-town-fights-back/

Crotty, James Marshall. (2012). *60% Of College Grads Can't Find Work In Their Field. Is A Management Degree The Answer?* Forbes Online. 1 March 2012. Web. Retrieved 7 August 2013. http://www.forbes.com/sites/jamesmarshallcrotty/2012/03/01/most-college-grads-cant-find-work-in-their-field-is-a-management-degree-the-answer/

Green, Charles. *Reasons for Small Business Failure.* The Houston Chronicle. Web. Retrieved 25 April 2013. http://smallbusiness.chron.com/reasons-small-businesses-failure-378.html

Matthews, Christopher. (2013). *With Baby-Boomers Retiring, Why Do We Need So Many Jobs?* Time: Business. 21 March 2013. Web. Retrieved 12 May 2013. http://business.time.com/2013/03/21/with-baby-boomers-retiring-why-do-we-need-so-many-new-jobs/

Merlevede, G., Vumum, G. *Choose a Career and Discover Your Perfect Job: 105 Tips on Work Attitude and Motivation.* Create Space Independent Publishing Platform. 2010, Print.

Purdy, Charles. *10 Words and Terms That Ruin a Resume.* Monster. Web. Retrieved 23 May 2013. http://career-advice.monster.com/resumes-cover-letters/resume-writing-tips/resume-killing-words-terms/article.aspx

Sample of job search and posting web-site at Monster: www.monster.com

Compensation data at Salary: www.salary.com

Spadafore, Anthony. *Now What?: The Young Person's Guide to Choosing the Perfect Career*. New York: Fireside Publishing. 2008, Print.

Toossi, Mitra. (2012). *Projections of the labor force to 2050: A Visual Essay*. Bureau of Labor Statistics. 14 October 2012. Web. Retrieved 24 March 2013. http://www.bls.gov/opub/mlr/2012/10/art1full.pdf

Occupational Outlook Handbook. Bureau of Labor Statistics. 29 March 2012. Web. Retrieved 18 March 2013. http://www.bls.gov/ooh/home.htm

Spending and Cash Flow

Anderson, Martha. *Budgeting for Newlyweds: The 5 Most Important Things You Can Do to Ensure a Financially Free Future With Your Spouse*. UGEI Publications. 2013, Kindle File.

Danko, William D., Stanley, Thomas J. *The Millionaire Next Door*. New York: Pocket Books. 1998. Print.

Dresden, Blake. *81 No Nonsense Ways to Save Money: Frugal Living Tips for the Resourceful Family*. Blake Dresden. 2013, Kindle File.

Keown, Arthur J. *Personal Finance: Turning Money into Wealth*. Upper Saddle River: Prentice Hall. 2012, Print.

Product selections at Consumer Reports:
Car valuations at Kelley Blue Book: www.kbb.com
Buying a home at National Association of Realtors: www.realtor.com
Home valuations, history, and price comparisons at Zillow: www.zillow.com or at Redfin: www.redfin.com

Richards, Charles Ph.D. (2012). *The Psychology of Wealth: Understand Your Relationship With Money and Achieve Prosperity*. New York: McGraw Hill. 17 January 2012, Print.

Various ratings of locales to live, work and play. http://www.bestplaces.net/docs/studies/

Debt Management

Clark, Ken. *The Complete Idiot's Guide to Getting Out of Debt*. New York: Alpha Books (Penguin Group). 2009, Print.

Credit scoring information at FICO: www.myfico.com
Credit counseling at National Foundation for Credit Counseling: www.nfcc.org

Edwards, B. , Rose, J. *Get Out of Debt Like The Debt Heroes: How 21 Ordinary People Paid Off Over 1.7 Million in Debt*. Money Smart Life Digital Publishing. 2013, Kindle File.

Greene, Mark. (2013). *A Look Behind the Curtain: How to Choose a Mortgage Lender*. Forbes. 26 March 2013. Web. Retrieved 22 August 2013. http://www.forbes.com/sites/moneybuilder/2013/03/26/a-look-behind-the-curtain-how-to-choose-a-mortgage-lender/

Stiglitz, Joseph E. (2013). *Student Debt and the Crushing of the American Dream*. New York Times: Opinionator. 12 May 2013. Web. Retrieved 20 May 2013. http://opinionator.blogs.nytimes.com/2013/05/12/student-debt-and-the-crushing-of-the-american-dream/

Student loan information at US Department of Education: http://studentaid.ed.gov/

7 Things Every Lender Considers (When Evaluating Your Small Business Loan Request). Match Finding. Web. Retrieved 22 August 2013. http://www.matchfinancing.com/business-loan-tips/2011/10/7-things-every-lender-considers-when-evaluating-your-small-business-loan-request/

Saving & Investing

Briody, Blaire. (2012). *5 Reasons Boomers Will Go Bust*. MSN: Money. 23 July 2012. Web. Retrieved 5 April 2013. http://money.msn.com/baby-boomers/5-reasons-boomers-will-go-bust-fiscaltimes.aspx

Wisenberg-Brin, Dinah. (2012). *Baby Boomers Are Ready For Retirement, Mostly*. CNBC. 17 April 2012. Web. Retrieved 19 May 2013. http://www.today.com/id/47063385/ns/today-today_news/t/baby-boomers-are-ready-retirement-mostly/#.UbhzS5xN_-4

Rating Mutual Funds and general investment informational site. http://www.morningstar.com

Good drill downs on financial topics, including saving and investing topics. http://www.mymoney.gov

Relationships

Robinson, Jonathan. *Communication Miracles for Couples: Easy and Effective Tools to Create More Love and Less Conflict.* San Francisco: Conari Press. 2012, Print.

Sayer, L.C., England, P., Allison, P., Kangas, N. (2010). *She Left, He Left: How Employment and Satisfaction Affect Men's and Women's Decisions to Leave Marriages.* American Journal of Sociology; 116:6, pp 1982-2018.

Dew, J., Britt, S. and Huston, S. (2012). *Examining the Relationship Between Financial Issues and Divorce.* Family Relations, 61: 615–628. doi: 10.1111/j.1741-3729.2012.00715.x School of Family Studies and Human Services, Kansas State University, Manhattan, KS 66506. Personal Financial Planning, Texas Tech University, Lubbock, TX 79409.

Philanthropy

Harper, Hill. (2012). *The Wealth Cure: Putting Money In Its Place.* New York: Gotham Books. 4 September 2012, Print.

10 Great Philanthropists Who Are Kids. 27 January 2011. Web. Retrieved 5 June 2013. http://listverse.com/2011/01/27/10-great-philanthropists-who-are-kids/

Contributions of Young Americans. American Red Cross. Web. Retrieved 12 June 2013. http://www.redcross.org/about-us/history/red-cross-american-history/contributions-young-americans

Corporation for National and Community Service. Web. Retrieved July 17 2013. http://www.serve.gov/

International Volunteer Facilitation and Placement. International Volunteer Headquarters. Web. Retrieved 10 June 2013. http://www.volunteerhq.org/

Our Mission. Teach for America. Web. Retrieved 25 May 2013. http://www.teachforamerica.org/our-mission

Volunteer. Volunteers of America. Web. Retrieved 6 May 2013. http://www.voa.org/Get-Involved/Volunteer

Risk Management

Attorney referrals - http://apps.americanbar.org/legalservices/lris/directory/

Certified Financial Planner referrals - http://www.cfp.net/utility/find-a-cfp-professional

CPA referrals - http://www.aicpa.org/FORTHEPUBLIC/FINDACPA/Pages/FindACPA.aspx

Fraud information at the National Fraud Information Center: www.fraud.org
Do it yourself legal forms and services at www.nolo.com
Tax rates, calculations and format at Internal Revenue Service: www.irs.gov

Referral portal to identify quality service providers and professionals within your region - http://www.angieslist.com

Healthcare Power of Attorney - American Bar Association. http://www.americanbar.org/content/dam/aba/uncategorized/2011/2011_aging_hcdec_univhcpaform.authcheckdam.pdf

Example of combined Healthcare Advanced Directive (used in Oregon). http://www.oregon.gov/DCBS/shiba/docs/advance_directive_form.pdf

Kaiser Health Tracking Poll. The Henry J. Kaiser Family Foundation. 19 June 2013. Web. Retrieved 25 June 2013. http://kff.org/health-reform/poll-finding/kaiser-health-tracking-poll-june-2013/

Selected Peterson Foundation Charts. The Peterson Foundation: Our America, Our Future. 7 May 2013. Web. Retrieved 1 June 2013. http://www.pgpf.org/sites/default/files/sitecore/media%20library/PGPF/Chart-Archive/PGPF-Chart-Pack.pdf

Thomas Insel. "*Mental Disorders as Brain Disorders: Thomas Insel at TED Talks*". YouTube video, 15:05, TED Talks: Caltech. 8 February 2012. http://www.youtube.com/watch?feature=player_embedded&v=u4m65sbqbhY#at=408

Why Is Health Spending In The US So High? Health at a Glance 2011: OECD Indicators. October 2011. Web. Retrieved 4 June 2013. http://www.oecd.org/els/health-systems/49084355.pdf

American Bar Association Guide to Wills and Estates, Fourth Edition: An Interactive Guide to Preparing Your Wills, Estates, Trusts, and Taxes. (American Bar Association Guide to Wills & Estates). Paperback by American Bar Association. Random House Reference; 4 edition (January 29, 2013)

Do it yourself simple estate planning toolkit. http://www.amazon.com/Alpha-Last-Will-Testament-Kit/dp/0937434388/ref=sr_1_3?s=books&ie=UTF8&qid=1375383039&sr=1-3&keywords=last+will+and+testament

Quicken WillMaker Plus 2013 Edition: Book & Software Kit Nolo; 2013 Edition edition (October 31, 2012)

INDEX

401k/403B, 84, 126, 135

A

activities, 6, 11, 74, 81, 95-96, 185, 188, 190-191
advisor, 140-141, 195
aging, 29-30, 34, 36, 127, 193
allocation, 136, 212
anxiety, 48, 113, 115, 189, 214
Apple, 33
archive, 10, 215, 220
asset class, 143-144, 146
associations, 11, 58, 191
athletic, 8-9
attire, 51
attitude, 46-47, 216
attorney, 166, 192-194, 213, 219
automate, 93, 181
automation, 1, 18, 21, 34

B

baby boom, 29
backup, 181
balance, 11, 18, 20, 25, 31-34, 43, 46, 51, 62, 71-72, 75, 77, 111-113, 117, 121, 127, 133, 174, 188, 191, 205
balance sheet, 117
bank, 108-109, 113, 116-117, 126, 210-211, 215
banker, 195
banking, 180, 195
BBB, 166, 213
better business bureau, 166, 196, 213
bonds, 136, 138, 143-144
borrow, 105-107, 113-114, 116
brand, 5, 7, 9-12, 39, 55, 57, 69, 78, 215
brokerage, 125, 135, 140, 142
brokers, 140-141
budget, 81, 91-94, 96, 117, 154, 157, 159, 168, 189, 194, 196

C

candidate, 46, 53-54, 70-71
capital, 21, 31-32, 44, 97, 106, 108, 146
car, 20, 47, 97, 99, 108, 110, 113, 163, 174, 176, 184, 193
career, 8-9, 48, 54, 60, 62-63, 66, 73-74, 76, 80-81, 99-100, 110, 121, 123, 127, 151, 169, 173, 184, 194, 201, 203, 214, 216

cars, 22, 123
cash, 33, 84, 91, 93-95, 99, 105, 108-110, 112, 126, 128, 135-136, 143, 146, 157, 159, 164, 174, 181, 217
cash flow, 84, 91, 93-95, 112, 128, 135, 146, 157, 159, 217
certified public accountant, 187
change, 17, 20, 22, 32-33, 38, 43, 46, 70, 75, 83-84, 139, 151, 158, 163, 179, 182, 204, 209-210, 212, 215
charity, 166-168, 187, 213
children, 151, 157-158, 166, 192-193
cliques, 73
closing, 54, 146
clothing, 10, 51, 107, 121
collaborate, 72
collaboration, 72, 79, 205
college, 37, 44, 47, 81, 95, 105, 110, 140, 158, 216
college debt, 110
commodities, 143-144
communications, 22, 34, 46, 51, 55, 60, 77, 90-91, 179, 215
community, 6, 8-9, 53-54, 80, 127, 159, 163-164, 166, 168, 195, 202, 219
compatibility, 10, 12, 153, 155

compensation, 5, 22, 25, 29, 45, 48, 52-53, 63, 76, 83-85, 124, 140-141, 166
compounding, 123, 125, 153
conflict, 78, 114, 154-155, 158, 194, 218
connectivity, 33, 82, 127
consumer, 38, 85, 91, 96-97, 105, 107, 113, 115, 134, 180, 212-213
consumer price index, 134
contractor, 60
cost of living, 89, 100, 153
counseling, 151, 189
coverage, 117, 128, 174-176, 213
CPA, 94, 187, 194, 219
CPI (inflation), 134
creative, 8, 75, 100, 165
credentials, 10, 53, 110, 195
crime, 100, 168, 178-179
cyber security, 178, 213
cybercrime, 178

D

debt, 101, 103, 105-108, 110-111, 113-114, 117, 211, 217
deductible, 176
demographics, 29, 36
dependency, 11, 37, 43, 121, 127-128
dependent, 19, 34, 43, 110, 128, 143, 151, 175

diet, 189
dilution, 11, 77
discipline, 12, 72, 79, 89, 91, 126, 159
diversification, 126, 134, 139, 143, 145
diversify, 134
drugs, 107, 154, 189-190

E

earn, 6, 48, 59, 81, 108, 112, 117, 133, 135-136, 188, 195
economy, 5, 12, 17-18, 20, 25, 29, 31, 35, 38-39, 111, 145, 203, 210, 215
education, 10, 21, 25, 29, 34, 37, 57, 80-81, 110, 112, 140, 154, 209, 215
efficiencies, 18, 29, 34, 36-37, 50, 77
efficiency, 19, 49, 204
ego, 45, 69, 90
elder, 36, 121, 123, 128, 134
email, 49-51, 55, 57-58, 60, 77, 106, 180, 182
employee, 10, 59-60, 62, 75, 82, 94, 124, 126
employer, 10, 46, 49, 53-55, 58-62, 69-71, 73, 75, 82-84, 95, 123, 125-127, 135, 174, 181, 185, 186

energy, 36, 38, 145, 210
entrepreneur, 61
eq, 78-79, 81
equities, 143
estate planning, 192, 194, 220
etf, 144
ethic, 21, 46, 71
exercise, 9, 92, 155, 165, 188-189
expertise, 72, 83, 140, 142, 146, 187, 193-195, 203

F

face value, 175
Facebook, 33
failure, 43, 53, 61, 112, 156, 196, 201-204, 210, 216
family, 1-2, 5-6, 8-9, 33, 43-44, 49, 78, 89, 95, 100, 106, 114, 123, 146, 151, 155, 157-159, 163, 165, 173-174, 179, 187, 192-193, 202, 217-218, 220
financing, 30, 95, 97, 105, 107, 109-110, 114
firewall, 179-180
foreign, 18-21, 31, 37, 138, 145
freelancing, 60-61
fuel, 29, 37-38
fun, 6, 43, 74, 89, 95, 121, 202, 206

G

gambling, 107, 190-191
GDP (gross domestic product), 35, 210
gift, 94, 164, 166-167
global, 1, 20-22, 31, 35, 38-39, 43, 127, 144-145, 210, 212
goals, 6-7, 9, 46, 62, 93, 127, 191, 205
GOOGLE, 33
governance, 32
government, 32, 43, 106, 111, 113, 126, 128, 169, 174, 184, 187, 192, 194
graduation, 1, 6-7, 47, 95, 105, 210-211, 215
gross domestic product (GDP), 35

H

Habitat for Humanity, 165
healthcare, 30, 62, 84, 145, 164, 174, 185, 188, 192-193, 219
hedge, 145
hedging, 145
humility, 81, 169, 205

I

image, 5, 10-11, 51, 59, 81, 97, 99, 163, 215
immigration, 21, 29-30
income, 44, 60, 63, 93-94, 112, 117, 125, 127-128, 135, 144, 151, 157-158, 167, 175, 184-185, 187
income statement, 117
index funds, 139
individual retirement account, 95, 124, 126
industrial, 33, 38, 51, 144
industries, 18, 44, 62, 138, 145, 201
inflation (CPI) 37-38, 134, 136, 212
innovation, 33, 35, 37-38, 45, 96
innovative, 31, 38, 146
innovators, 32-33, 35-37
installment credit, 113
insurance, 60, 84, 97, 100, 109, 140, 174-176, 190, 194, 214
insure, 82, 174, 176
integrity, 10, 31, 46, 205
interest, 6, 36, 44, 49, 52, 55, 57, 59, 63, 97, 107, 109-111, 113-114, 116, 123, 133, 143-144, 146, 151, 158, 185
interest expense, 97
interest rates, 44, 107, 111, 113-114, 116
internet, 17, 22, 31, 33, 145, 179
interview, 5, 47, 51-53, 56, 58, 71, 165

invest, 25, 49, 99, 125-126, 129, 133, 139, 143, 145-146
investment, 31, 33, 37, 76, 81, 105, 109-110, 117, 124-126, 131, 133-143, 145-147, 156, 195, 212, 218
investor, 35, 123-124, 134, 136, 138, 142-143, 145-146, 205
IQ, 78
IRA (individual retirement account), 95, 126, 135
IRS (internal revenue service), 124-125, 185-186, 194

J

job, 1, 5, 10, 17-20, 25, 29, 36-37, 43-57, 59-63, 65-67, 69, 71-85, 99-101, 108-111, 117, 121, 123, 127, 158, 165, 174, 195, 203, 209-212, 216

L

labor, 16, 18-22, 29-30, 34, 63, 74, 82, 173, 210, 212-213, 216
lender, 106, 109, 113, 115-117, 217-218
leverage, 34, 50, 55, 58-59, 164, 177, 194, 202
life cycle accounts, 139

lifestyle, 89, 91, 96, 98, 100-101, 107, 124, 168
loans, 105, 107, 109-114, 116, 211, 215
location, 100, 145, 166
loyalty, 20, 62, 127

M

marketers, 91
Maslow, 90-91
master, 59, 75, 215
mastery, 75, 83, 202-203, 205
meals on wheels, 165
Medicare, 30, 209
mental health, 188-189, 214
mentor, 95
mentoring, 168
millionaire, 38, 98, 210, 217
mobility, 12, 21, 62, 82
mortgage, 44, 97, 109, 156, 195, 217
multi-tasking, 77, 190
mutual funds, 138-139, 141, 218

N

net worth, 105, 117
network, 50, 55-56, 80, 178-179
networking, 33, 47, 50, 59, 73, 80, 100
non-profit, 125, 165, 167, 187, 194

O

obesity, 188
outsource, 63
overseas, 20-21, 31, 38, 178

P

pace, 32, 36, 62, 101
passion, 76, 204
passionate, 164
password, 179-181
past due, 111-112
pawn, 70, 114
pay, 5, 10, 17, 20, 33, 44, 52-53, 59, 63, 69, 85, 95, 100, 105, 108, 110, 112-115, 117, 121, 124, 128, 135, 140-141, 143, 156, 175-176, 178, 184-185, 187-188, 193, 195
pay rate, 52, 124
paycheck, 41, 84, 95, 110, 126
payday, 110, 124
payday loans, 110
payroll, 60, 85, 94, 126, 128, 164, 168, 185
pension, 124
perceived wealth, 127
performance, 19, 37, 72, 75, 77-79, 108, 133, 135-136, 139, 141, 145, 166
perseverance, 205

personal financial statement, 116-117
personal loans, 114
pets, 97
pettiness, 73
phone, 49-51, 54-55, 58, 60, 77, 90, 94, 154, 163, 179, 181
physical health, 188-189
planner, 6, 141, 194, 214, 219
planning, 1, 6-7, 63, 80, 93, 117, 127, 135, 140, 153, 159, 184, 192, 194, 206, 215, 218, 220
policies, 174-176
political, 1-2, 20, 151
politics, 2, 20
population, 30, 36, 114, 215
power, 18, 31-35, 47, 70, 78, 123, 125, 134, 145, 165, 192-193, 199, 201, 203-205, 209, 219
power of attorney, 192-193, 219
precious metals, 143-144
premium, 31, 70, 136, 174-176, 185
presentation, 51, 180
price, 5, 12, 95-97, 109, 134, 142-145, 179
pricing, 38, 100, 116, 143, 195
prima donna, 81
privacy, 114, 116, 154, 158, 180, 182

private, 78, 84, 114, 116, 146, 154, 158, 178-180, 182, 203
process, 18, 21, 30-31, 37, 48, 50-51, 53-54, 56, 71, 74-75, 80, 84, 93-94, 116, 123, 133, 157, 168-169, 185, 186-187, 193-194, 204, 206
productivity, 18, 29, 77, 189
professional, 18, 34, 44, 52, 59, 76, 134, 138, 146, 157, 166, 195-196, 203
professionalism, 46
profit, 18, 21, 37-38, 125, 165, 167, 187, 194

R

race, 1, 211
real estate, 143, 146
recession, 17, 25, 31, 69, 145, 215
reconcile, 181
recruiter, 45, 59-60, 63
reference, 48-49, 58, 82, 91, 116, 185, 193, 220
references, 49, 58, 84
registered tax return preparer, 187, 194
REIT (real estate investment trust), 143
relationship, 1-2, 11, 58-59, 84, 142, 151, 153-154, 156-158, 188, 201, 217-218

religious, 1-2
rent, 97, 108-110, 113, 121, 154
resources, 11, 18, 31-33, 58-59, 82, 117, 145, 153-154, 159, 164, 166, 186, 192-193, 195-196, 205, 213, 215, 217, 219
resume, 45, 48-51, 53, 55-57, 84, 113, 165, 216
retire, 6, 85, 121, 127, 134
retirement, 29, 62, 95, 97, 123-128, 134-135, 142, 145, 158, 210, 212, 215, 218
return on investment, 76, 134-135
revolving credit, 114
risk, 12, 18, 32, 46, 59, 70, 73, 98, 113, 115-117, 134-136, 142, 144-146, 157, 159, 173-174, 178-179, 188, 190, 202, 212, 219
robotics, 18
ROI (return on investment), 76, 134
roommate, 95, 154

S

sales, 25, 61, 63, 145, 185
saving, 43, 99, 121, 123, 127, 129, 135, 180, 212, 218
savings, 38, 62, 69, 84, 94-95, 97, 109, 121, 123-129, 133, 135, 140, 168, 176, 193-194, 212

school, 1-2, 25, 30, 37, 47, 53, 57, 61, 72, 105, 110-111, 123, 157, 168, 173, 201, 210, 215, 218

schools, 21, 98, 111, 163, 184

security, 5-6, 10, 17, 30, 74, 90, 95, 106, 116, 124, 128, 141, 144, 175, 177-178, 180-181, 185, 204, 212-213

self starter, 82

senses, 51, 180

skills, 10, 47, 57, 60, 63, 69-70, 72, 78, 80, 82, 138, 153-155, 165, 169, 189, 203, 215

social, 5, 33-34, 37, 43, 50, 69, 73, 78, 80-81, 90, 100-101, 124, 128, 151, 159, 163, 168, 175, 180-181, 184-185, 187, 189, 204, 212

social causes, 80, 159

social networking, 33, 50, 73, 100

social security, 124, 128, 175, 181, 185, 212

social services, 43, 163, 168

solicit, 167

specialists, 20, 195

specialization, 19

spend, 7, 57, 89, 91-92, 94-95, 99, 101, 117, 127, 129, 141, 157-158, 169, 185, 206

spending, 38, 43, 74, 85, 89-91, 94-96, 99, 117, 127-128, 159, 168, 193, 211, 217, 220

spiritual, 8-9, 78

staffing, 20-21, 59, 211

stock, 33, 124, 126-127, 138-139, 143, 145, 189

struggle, 1, 9, 17, 190, 192, 196, 199, 201, 203, 205

success, 1, 5-6, 9, 11-12, 17, 31, 36, 45, 48, 59, 61, 73, 75, 81, 83, 98, 133, 191, 201, 203-206, 214

supervisor, 22, 78

sustainable, 17, 38

T

talent, 21

tariff, 20

tax, 30, 37, 60, 124-125, 168, 184-188, 190-191, 194

taxes, 60, 85, 94-95, 97, 109, 125, 128, 135, 184-185, 186-187, 194, 220

TCO(total cost of owner ship), 97

team, 31, 46, 53, 72-73, 79, 138-139, 165, 205

teamwork, 46, 72

technologies, 19, 21, 31, 33-34, 37, 77, 90, 127

technology, 33, 36, 57, 145, 179-180, 191, 209
temp agencies, 49, 59
term, 2, 10-11, 60, 84, 98, 117, 126, 133-136, 142, 151, 155, 166-167, 175, 182, 195
terminate, 124
terminated, 43, 174
termination, 174, 192
terms, 1, 53, 78, 83, 108, 111, 113, 115, 216
tools, 34, 50, 53, 76-77, 81, 126, 210, 212, 218
total compensation, 84
total cost of ownership (TCO), 97
trade, 20-21, 37, 58, 115, 212
training, 21, 34
transformation, 31-32, 73
tribal, 31
trojan horse, 179
trust, 7, 46, 59, 114, 143, 146, 155, 168, 180, 192-193, 205, 209

U

unemployment, 20, 22, 25, 29, 41, 43
united way, 168
utility, 72

V

valuation, 33
value, 2, 5, 33, 38, 45, 47, 50, 71, 78, 80-82, 84, 96, 101, 105, 107-109, 114, 116, 135, 144-145, 175, 185
visa, 21
vision, 6-9, 11-12, 22, 39, 62, 72, 79, 100, 155
volatility, 134-136, 143
volunteer, 164-165, 213, 219

W

wages, 1, 18, 124
wealth, 6, 33, 38-39, 61, 98, 105, 127, 155, 167, 185, 187, 193, 210, 215, 217, 219
will, 191-193
work, 5-6, 18, 20-22, 25, 31, 43, 45-48, 52-53, 55, 57, 59-60, 62, 66, 69-74, 76, 78-79, 82, 85, 93, 98-99, 112, 116, 121, 123-124, 126-127, 129, 133, 140, 146, 153-154, 156-158, 175-177, 188-189, 191, 204-205, 216-217
workforce, 18, 29-30, 37, 127, 209-210, 215
workplace, 12, 43, 69, 72-75, 78-82, 168

ABOUT THE AUTHOR

Over a 30 year consulting career, Paul Nourigat has advised families, businesses, and community leaders across the country. In addition to his time spent with thousands of highly successful people, he has invested extensive time with families who are struggling with money.

As a result, Paul developed a clear understanding of "what works" and "what doesn't" in business and personal finance. While he benefited from that knowledge, it became clear that others needed the knowledge and context for that knowledge earlier in life, in order to avoid painful financial mistakes. Having heard over and over "I wish I knew then what I know now", Paul set out on a mission to teach young Americans about money using a very unique approach.

Commissioning over 600 pieces of original art, his first 8 books are fictional and visual showcases for pre-20 eyes, breaking new ground teaching financial literacy in his recent Graphic Novel "If Money Could Shout: the brutal truths for teens".

Moving onto the non-fiction format of "No Time To Wander: the financial compass for young Americans", he demonstrates his awareness that people in their 20's and 30's want direct knowledge and straight answers. Through candor and crystallizing core financial concepts, he believes readers will be empowered to pursue multiple exciting paths in their life journey, culminating in financial security.

Discover more about Paul and his titles at
www.FarBeyond.com and www.facebook.com/paul.nourigat

FarBeyond Publishing
"Messages to last a lifetime"